The Illum

MW01292654

Deception, ~~~, ~~~~~~ ~ Assassinations by the World's Most Powerful Secret Society

By

Frank White

Table of Contents

Introduction

The world is being fashioned and shaped right in front of our very own eyes, yet 85% of the world's population has absolutely no clue to how this is being done and who is doing the actual molding and shaping and what their aim and agenda truly is. However, there are people who make up the remaining 15% who do know what exactly is going on. You can split this remaining 15% into two separate and distinct groups. They are the 10% and the 5%.

The 10% group are the holders of knowledge that enslave the 85% by keeping them ignorant of what's really going on in the world by using the sinister tools of programming, manipulation and brainwashing. The top tier or the elite of this 10% group are the Illuminati and they have created and operate out of a hierarchal compartmentalized pyramid structure which sole purpose is to bring forth the Global agenda.

It is a compartmentalized pyramid structure simply because each layer of the pyramid (except for those who are at the top) does not know what is going on in the other layers. The people who work for the entities in each of these layers are just simply there to perform a function and carry out orders issued to them by the people at the top of the pyramid and they are not privy to what the Global agenda is. They are told only enough information so that they can do their job.

For example, if you are a bank teller and you work for either Bank of America or JP Morgan Chase, you're working for an entity that comprises the Banking layer of this pyramid structure which was created by the Illuminati and you probably didn't know that until now. All you had on your mind was applying for a job that would allow you to feed, clothe and shelter your family. When you got hired, you got hired to perform a function of the bank. Within another pyramid scheme you are at the bottom layer.

You probably also weren't aware of the fact the Illuminati bloodlines of the Rockefeller and the Rothschilds own and control these particular entities. But how would you actually know this when the Rockefellers and the Rothschilds own entities through a multitude of trusts? This information is not exactly broadcasted to the public. The major banks appear to be in competition with each other, but this is nothing more than an illusion and a complete sham because they are really connected and form the banking cartel which the Rothschilds are the head of.

Other entities that also comprise these layers and operate out of this aforementioned pyramid structure in which the Illuminati are the capstone are the transnational corporations, the military, the educational system, government and politics, the media, religion, entertainment, organized crime, other secret societies and the intelligence agencies like the CIA, Mossad, and MI6.

The 5% group which I mentioned a little bit earlier and which I consider myself a proud member of are the people who have the clairvoyance to analyze and dissect the inner workings of this pyramid structure and decipher what the Illuminati's global agenda truly is and in many cases like mine in particular, are not afraid to reveal what we've have uncovered and expose it the masses of people who simply don't know what's going on and as a result are sinking in the quicksand of ignorance.

Therefore, my ultimate goal in writing this particular book entitled **The Illuminati's Greatest Hits: Deception, Conspiracies, Murders And Assassinations By The World's Most Powerful Secret Society** is to expose the truth to the masses of how the world in which we live in is being shaped and fashioned by a small diabolical group of people known as the Illuminati who operate from the shadows and have toppled countries and their leaders not only through the acts of deception, corruption, and theft, but also through flat out murder and assassinations, all in the name of creating a New World Order which is their global agenda.

In this book I will cover the major historical figures from various time periods who simply stood in the way of the Illuminati and their New World Order Global Empire Machine or flat out rejected its overtures and as a result were assassinated.

Illuminati Primer

Before we dive into the Illuminati's Greatest Hits it's very important that you become familiar with the origins of the world's most powerful secret society, the organizations in which they operate out of to bring forth their New World Order agenda, the interconnecting 13 Illuminati bloodlines and their quest for world domination. So here is an Illuminati primer.

The Illuminati was founded on May 1, 1776, by Adam Weishaupt who was funded by the Rothschilds and a professor of Canon Law at the University of Ingolstadt in Bavaria, Germany. Weishaupt was a Jew who converted to Roman Catholicism and became a Jesuit priest. He later broke from the Catholic Church to form the Illuminati which was originally known as the Perfectibilists or "the perfect ones" as their goal was to create a perfect world in which all men and women were equal, and the Catholic Church had no say over the government. The sun became their symbol represented by a circle with a dot in the middle and rays emanating around the circle.

Weishaupt later adopted the name Illuminati which means "the enlightened ones" and modeled this secret society after Freemasonry. In fact, Weishaupt used his newly formed organization to infiltrate the Masonic lodges with the goal of placing Illuminati members in the positions of power.

Members were considered freethinkers and included many prominent people at the time such as Ferdinand of Brunswick, the diplomat Xavier von Zwack (second-in-command of the order), literary men Johann Wolfgang von Goethe and Johann Gottfried Herder, and the Dukes of both Weimar and Gotha. Members took a vow of secrecy and pledged allegiance to the order, its tenets and its superiors.

However, Karl Theodor the ruler of Bavaria at the time with the blessing of the Catholic Church banned the Illuminati as well as other secret societies. Weishaupt fled the country on horseback and while fleeing he dropped some documents that laid out the plans of the Illuminati which included overthrowing the monarchies of Europe. Weishaupt eventually escaped to Gotha where he was given refuge by Duke Ernst II of Saxe - Gotha – Altenberg. Weishaupt eventually died in Gotha in 1811.

History says the Illuminati disbanded in 1785, however, they had members located all throughout Europe and the United States and simply went underground hell bent on bringing in their New World Order which phrase is symbolically printed on the reverse side of the United States Seal and the dollar bill with the Latin words "Novus Ordo Seclorum" which technically translates to "a new order of the ages." I get much deeper into the symbolism that the Illuminati use to communicate and are obsessed with in my book entitled **Who Are The Illuminati: The Secret Societies, Symbols, Bloodlines and The New World Order**.

So what exactly is the New World Order? Well basically it's a sinister and a diabolical plan by the Global elite headed by the 13 Illuminati bloodlines and their offshoots whose New World Order agenda includes the bringing into existence of:

- A one world government
- A one world army
- One global currency

- One central bank
- A micro-chipped mind controlled enslaved population in the so-called technetronic era as stated by Zbigniew Brezezinksi in his book Between Two Ages: America's Role in the Technetronic Era
- A complete totalitarian state

Now that you know what the New World Order agenda is here are the 13 bloodlines that make up the Illuminati.

1. The Rockefeller Bloodline
2. The Rothschild Bloodline
3. The Kennedy Bloodline
4. The Astor Bloodline
5. The Bundy Bloodline
6. The Collins Bloodline
7. The DuPont Bloodline
8. The Freeman Bloodline
9. The Li Bloodline
10. The Onassis Bloodline
11. The Reynolds Bloodline
12. The Russell Bloodline
13. The Van Duyn Bloodline

The Rothschilds are considered to be the most powerful among the bloodlines as it is said that they own half of the world's wealth and historians and researchers say they are worth approximately 500 trillion dollars. They also own nearly all of the central banks in the world including the Federal Reserve located in the United States that's neither federal nor do they have any reserves. The Federal Reserve is a private banking cartel that controls the US money supply and doesn't have anything to do with the United States government except for the fact United States has to borrow from the Fed every time it needs money. In fact, money can't come into existence without the Federal Reserve.

The Rothschilds also make their money by funding both sides in pretty much every war and charging huge interest payments on the money that they loan. They are in essence considered the wizards of finance and at one time they were responsible for setting the price of gold through their company NM Rothschild.

The Rockefellers are currently led by David Rockefeller and they have many companies and interests. John D. Rockefeller founded the monopoly Standard Oil which in the early 1880's controlled 90% of US refineries and pipelines. He once stated that "competition is a sin". In 1911, the Supreme Court ruled that Standard Oil violated the antitrust laws and ordered it to dissolve, but basically what the Rockefellers did was create different companies using various trusts. The new companies were named Mobil Oil, Amoco and Exxon.

David Rockefeller is primarily responsible for creating and funding some of the organizations that the Illuminati use a conduit to shape global affairs and carry out the New World Order agenda. These organizations include the Trilateral Commission and the Council on Foreign Relations who prominent members include Henry Kissinger, George Soros, Zbigniew Brzezinski, Dick Cheney, Robert Rubin, and Hillary Clinton. Other organizations that are used as a conduit to shape global affairs and carry out the New World Order agenda are The Club of Rome, The Bilderberg Group, The Committee of 300, The Round Table Group, The Royal Institute of International Affairs, and The Tavistock Institute. They also use so called philanthropic foundations like the Rockefeller and Ford foundation to fund causes that promote their New World Order agenda. In addition to this they are using the United Nations to form their goal of a one world government and are using NATO to create the stated one world army. Proof of this is when NATO (the world army) bombed Libya which I will cover later on.

In **Who Are The Illuminati: The Secret Societies, Symbols, Bloodlines and The New World Order** I go into further details about the 13 bloodlines of the Illuminati, their ties to Satanism, and I also cover in greater detail the aforementioned front organizations, its members and show how everything is all interconnected.

Now that you have a basic understanding of the Illuminati and their New World Order agenda let's examine the ruthless and murderous way in which they go about implementing this agenda by killing those major historical figures who have opposed them and attempted to get in the way of their Global empire juggernaut.

Chapter 1: The French Revolution and the Execution of Louis XVI

In the Spring of 1789, feudal France is divided in three unequal castes. At the top were the nobility, headed by the King of France, Louis the XVI, grandson of the iconic Louis the XIV, a prominent Illuminati nicknamed the Sun King. Also at the top of the caste during this time were the military. Below the nobility are the clergy who range in power from Cardinals to rural priests. France in 1789 by the way is almost exclusively Catholic, with the exception of a few Jewish citizens. And at the bottom are the Tiers-État, the Third State; these are the commoners, the peasants, the merchants, the workers and the serfs.

After centuries of servitude, the Tiers-État is finally waking up to the inequalities, and the French Revolution is brewing. But are they waking up on their own?

Taking a look at the origins of Illuminism, we see that it was a secret revolutionary society behind freemasonry. The Illuminati penetrated into all the lodges of Grand Orient Freemasonry, and were backed and organized by cabalistic Jews. It is interesting to note that the Duc D'Orleans and Charles Maurice de Talleyrand were both initiated into Illuminism by Mirabeau shortly after the latter had introduced it into France, from Frankfurt, where its headquarters had been established in 1782 under Adam Weishaupt.

Adam Weishaupt, founder of Bavarian Illuminized Masonry, an emissary of the Rothschilds, was a member of the Masonic Grand Orient in 1784. This was the time Illuminism made its grand entrance in France. Of 282 Masonic lodges in Paris by 1789, 266 lodges were controlled by the Illuminati. Weishaupt had sent a letter to a man named Maximillien Robespierre in

Paris, urging him to start the French Revolution. However, the messenger was struck by lightning and killed during his voyage from Frankfurt to Paris. When police searched his body, they found the letter and stifled the uprising attempt.

With this in mind, it should come as no surprise that the convention in Paris was the catalyst of the "Revolution".

Indeed, in 1785, one of the largest Freemason conventions in the world was held in Paris. Coincidence? A secret committee was set up at the Masonic convention in February 1785 to coordinate the actions of the Revolution. It included Saint-Martin, Etrilla, Franz Anton Mesmer, Cagliostro, Mirabeau, Charles Maurice de Talleyrand, Bode, Dahlberg, the Baron de Gleichen, Lavater, Count Louis de Hesse, and representatives of the Grand Orient from Poland and Lithuania. And of course Weishaupt. Weishaupt always played a leading role at the Illuminati's meetings in Paris, even from afar. All of these names will come back prominently during and after the French Revolution.

Rumors had been circulating that Louis the XVI was a tyrannical simpleton, ruthlessly ruling the land and wanting nothing but the unhappiness of the Tiers-État.

Louis the XVI was widely misunderstood due to an extreme vision problem. His shortsightedness was so bad he would often not recognize even his own advisors until they were mere feet away. This led him to be generally quiet in large groups, resulting in people thinking he was too intimidated to talk, and not fit for the task of public speaking. On the contrary, the King was a gentle man who wanted nothing more than the people's happiness. Indeed, he abolished many of the oppressive measures that had been prevalent until then in the country, paving a way of sorts for the Revolutionaries to obtain what they wanted.

Louis the XVI had actually abolished torture in 1788, reformed the judicial system, humanized the treatment of prisoners, and instituted a health system. He also facilitated over 40,000 kilometers of paved road, the envy of most developed European nations. Industry and agriculture were booming, and exports had been decupled over the reign of Louis the XVI alone. Contrary to popular belief today, and to the propaganda fed the inhabitants of the country at the time, the Revolution was not fomented in a destitute country but in a flourishing nation with a strong economy.

At the same time, Marie-Antoinette, Louis the XVI's Austrian wife, was also misunderstood. Her childhood had been rigid and her upbringing severe. While she ended up speaking French, this was not her language of choice. Why does this matter? Well, she was seen by her French subjects as being distant and unwilling to discuss matters of importance with them. She became an easy target.

By the Spring of 1789, pamphlets mocking the Queen began circulating. They openly made her look like a deranged woman, out of touch with reality. It was easy for the people to start hating a woman who allegedly would have said of rioters demanding more affordable flour and bread in front of the Castle of Versailles, "Let them eat cake." She quickly became a symbol of evil in the land, thanks to a well-oiled propaganda machine.

In this unstable climate, the Illuminati took advantage of their positions of power to spread rumors and falsities about the King and the Queen. The ultimate goal was of course to get them dethroned.

By 1788, a group of hard-core freemasons, calling themselves the Jacobins, were in charge of the Revolutionary committees across Paris and the province. The Jacobins were organized in clubs with such poetic names as Les Amis Réunis (The Reunited Friends). The Jacobins had a centralized network over all France. The first club was taken over by Weishaupt's close collaborators Bode and Baron de Busche. The coup was in motion and soon, the 152 active Jacobins clubs were under Illuminati influence.

In May 1789, the States General, a meeting where representatives of each cast was invited to offer their grievances, were called. The purpose was to quiet down the spirits. Why did the people need to be quieted down?

In July 1788, a series of catastrophic weather events had sent hail storms across the plains of Beauce, the grain elevator of France at the time. Harvests spoiled under the heavy rains, trees were uprooted due to the high winds and vineyards were destroyed. To add to the already skyrocketing prices of flour and grain, the winter 1788-1789 was especially brutal, resulting in harbors in the Mediterranean Sea freezing over, putting an abrupt halt to trading and commerce. The English Channel froze as well, an extremely rare occurrence, and no exchanges happened with England and the northern European countries that winter. Mills were halted due to the streams freezing as well, and suddenly the price of ground flour and bread quadrupled. Over 100,000 people were dislodged from their homes, sent walking around the countryside in hopes of finding food and striking their fortune.

These events made it easy for the instigators of the Revolution to frighten the populace and make them believe their very existence was in danger, not due to climatic conditions, but in reality due to the regime's inability to protect them. How gullible and malleable are crowds in times of despair!

But the fact remained that the people were angry and looking for justice, a reason for their demise, an explanation.

On March 1st, 1789, a young Corsican lieutenant, Napoleon Bonaparte, was sent to Dijon to crush some riots. Instead of defending the King's interests, he took the side of the revolutionaries and became an essential instrument of the Revolution and the period thereafter.

On July 14, 1789, any history book will tell you that the French Revolution was started. Of course, this is simplistic. The Prise de la Bastille, the moment where 200 angry revolutionaries, led by Illuminati, took over the prison of the Bastille, is a symbolic moment but had really no influence whatsoever on what was going on. On the 13th of July 1789, at 11 PM, some conspirators gathered at the church of Prix Saint-Antoine where they set up Comité Révolutionnaire, a revolutionary committee and discussed how to organize the revolutionary militia. It will come as no surprise that Dufour, from the Grand Orient, chaired the meeting.

Despite having only seven prisoners in its cells at the time, prisoners who by the way were well treated and in good health, it was elevated on a pedestal to become an iconic event. The mob that attacked the prison, led by Camille DesMoulins, in a rash moment, decapitated the prison's administrator and paraded his severed head on a spike on the streets of Paris, as a sign of victory over the oppression of the "power".

This iconic event served as the momentum the Illuminati had been looking for to encourage the people to rise and riot. Almost instantly, bloodshed ensued. To the cries of "Liberté, Égalité, Fraternité" (Liberty, Equality, Fraternity), the Revolution raged on as Illuminati emissaries were sent all over the land to spread the word that the Revolution had started. The panic set forth was unprecedented. The people were led to believe that bands of dislodged and angry bandits were roaming the countryside, making any travel unsafe, and threatening the very existence of every honest person in the realm. They were depicted as going from village to village, pillaging and ravaging the homes of farmers and serfs to find the slightest bit of food.

The seemingly worthy causes of "Liberté, Égalité, Fraternité" (Liberty, Equality, Fraternity) were in reality the Illuminati agenda.

The word *"Liberty"* to Illuminism means liberty of man from God, the liberty of man to do as he wants, when he wants, free of the shackles of the Christian religion. Rebellion and anarchy are to be used to achieve such liberty.

"Equality," meanwhile, implies that all authority is to be smashed and that no man should own more goods than his fellows. Man would have little or no property to tie him down, no family or children, no cities, no government. Instead, rewilded man would live pure in nature in a savage and primitive, yet exalted, state.

"Fraternity" means that all men are to be brothers, the artificial strictures of national borders, religions, and races, etc. obliterated.

To attain these goals, any means were to be employed. Mirabeau once proclaimed, "What matter the means as long as one arrives at the end?" - the same end-justifies-the-means philosophy preached from Weishaupt to Lenin to Hitler.

"Royal decrees" started circulating that it was OK to burn castles and steal from the aristocrats, the upper cast, with impunity. With a fake royal seal, these decrees look every bit official, and peasants looking to appease their desire for justice did not look further into the fakes. The nobility became a habitual target. Pillaging their castles, manors and residences, stealing anything of value and destroying the rest, the Revolution impoverished the Nobles.

People in the provinces are encouraged to attack the military arsenals to seize their weapons. This period is called La Grande

Peur, the Great Fear, due to the terror that crawled across the nation as fast as horses could reach the next village.

On August 4, 1789, it was voted to abolish all privileges. All men became equal under the law. This was the de facto end of the caste system in France; it was the end of the Ancient Régime, the Old Regime, meaning the Absolute Monarchy, and its God-given King.

The National Assembly was moved into an old horse manège on the Rue de Rivoli in October 1789. The radicals sat to the left of the chairman, the conservatives to the right. Hence the Illuminati invented left and right as ideological concepts in world politics. Everything that had to do with the left was thereafter considered progressive since it was true Illuminism.

By October 1789, the royal family was removed from Versailles, the royal palace, and moved to Paris, in some comfortable but lesser apartments. It was the sign that under the new Constitutional Monarchy, the capital of the country was to be Paris again.

By then, Louis the XVI had realized that he was being kept alive for appearances only, and knew that his time was to come soon.

So in the night of June 20 to June 21, 1791, Louis the XVI, his wife Marie Antoinette and their children, tried to flee Paris for Varennes, a small town southeast of Paris. Unfortunately, their coach was stopped and it was said that they had wanted to start a counter-revolution. The angry mob was infuriated and captured the King, accusing him of treason.

Every revolution has its leaders. The leaders of the French Revolution of 1789 were all Illuminati. The names Marat, Danton, Robespierre, DesMoulins, Mirabeau, all became synonymous with power and force. After taking over the Jacobin clubs, they started wearing Phrygian Caps, the red symbol of freedom. Indeed, the Phrygian cap is a soft conical cap with the top pulled forward, associated in antiquity with the inhabitants of Phrygia, a region of central Anatolia. In the western provinces of the Roman Empire it came to signify freedom and the pursuit of liberty, perhaps through a case of mistaken identity with the "pileus," the felt cap of emancipated slaves of ancient Rome.

At any rate, red caps started popping up all over Paris and soon all over France, a sure way to recognize those in favor of the Revolution. Interestingly enough, red is also the predominant color of the banner of the House of Rothschild.

But back to the King, in the custody of an angry mob, his escape attempt was seen as a profound dichotomy between the people and its ruler. The people were divided on this issue, as on so many others. Riot ensued and martial law was declared. The Terreur, the Reign of Terror, had its first precursor.

Brutal retaliation against the rioters by the revolutionaries Danton, Robespierre and Marat force people to choose sides. Every sympathizer to the cause is now to be referred to as a Citoyen, a citizen. The worst thing at that time would be to be referred to as a Ci-Devant, referring to the article or pronoun in the aristocrats' names. Ironically, most of the prominent figures of the Revolution were aristocrats themselves!

A new flag came into use during this period. It is the traditional tricolor flag France still has now, the Blue, White and Red flag. White is the traditional color of the House of Bourbon, who ruled in France from the late 16th Century until the French Revolution. On the flag, the color white represents the King. Officially, the red and blue in the flag represents the city of Paris.

Revolutionaries in Paris traditionally flew red and blue. Likewise, revolutionaries wore blue and red cockades (ribbons) on their hats during the Revolution.

To cut their ties with everything related to the monarchy, the revolutionaries decided to change many current symbols that had been in place for centuries. Among the changes, the metric system was introduced and pushed to an extreme. By 1793, the year was now divided in 12 months renamed after nature and the seasons. Each month counted three equal 10-day periods, and the additional 5 days found the year were de facto holidays. But the name of the months was not the only change that occurred in the calendar. In addition, 1792 became retroactively An 1, or Year 1. To sever all ties with religion meant to start a calendar that did not count down from the death of Jesus.

Despite all the riffs between the castes, France had been growing until then. The Revolution brought about an age of famine and poverty. It was even said that the Duke of Orleans, grand master of the Grand Orient Lodge of Freemasons, reportedly bought all the grain in 1789 and either sold it abroad or hid it away, thus creating near starvation among commoners. By the way, the Grand Orient Freemasonry worked under the Illuminati, and under that again the Blue, or National, Masonry had operated until it was converted over-night into Grand Orient Masonry by Phillipe d'Orléans in 1773. D'Orléans even renamed himself Philippe Égalité, or Philippe Equality, under the guise of being a sympathizer to the cause, hoping to escape the revolutionaries' wrath.

Galart de Montjoie, a contemporary, blamed the Revolution almost solely on the Duke of Orleans, adding that he "was moved by that invisible hand which seems to have created all the events of our revolution in order to lead us towards a goal that we do not see at present..."

The prosperity the country had been enjoying up until the Revolution was now long gone. The Terreur was established as a legitimate (or so they wanted the people to think) way of ruling the country. The Commune was established in 1792 and citizens were punished for the most trivial deviances from the rulers' ideology. At one point, 144 seamstresses were killed in Nantes. Their crime? They had sewn shirts for the rebels...

People were executed without trial, despite the ostensible introduction of so-called revolutionary tribunals in September 1789. One of the judges presiding at these trials was the perverted Marquis Donatien Alphonse Francois de Sade, who had been brought straight from a mental hospital. De Sade was responsible for giving the concept "sadism" a name. As a sign of his unstable nature, it must be noted that he also died in a mental hospital. So in short, he was brought out of treatment for a short but deadly period of time, to conduct the regime's dirtiest jobs.

To make the executions more efficient, Docteur Guillotin introduced his now infamous invention, later named after him, the guillotine. The sharp blade was designed to drop down so fast that it could kill people faster, with less effort. Charles Henri Sanson, the chief executor, holds the macabre record of having cut off 21 heads in 38 minutes.

The Commune leadership was comprised of 288 Illuminati, including Danton and Robespierre. Les Enragés (the Enraged) wanted to radically eliminate everyone who had shown any kind of misgivings about the Revolution.

Anatole France, a famous French writer, said in his book "Les Dieux ont soif" ("The Thirsty Gods"), "The Gods are thirsty, not for power, but for blood." He best summarized the Reign of Terror, and how the extremism Danton, a definite rogue, and now Minister of Justice, was taken to the next level.

For many, their status was enough to make them guilty. Priests and aristocrats, that is those who had not emigrated under the threat of the regime, were automatically guilty. Their assets were seized and divided between the leaders themselves and the nation's coffers. In Paris alone, over 2,800 people were assassinated between September 2, 1792 and September 4, 1792.

The Jacobins started shutting down the Masonic Lodges that were not of any use to them anymore. By 1794, there were only 12 lodges left, the ones of course the most loyal to the Illuminati agenda.

Philippe Égalité was guillotined despite having renounced his title and in 1792, leaving his position as Grand Master of the Grand Orient, which he had held for 20 years since the founding of the Order. He knew too much about the preparations for the Revolution. He had worked closely with the Jacobins in the hope that he might be allowed to take the throne as a constitutional monarch.

Philippe Égalité explained why he left the Grand Orient in the following manner, "I no longer know who belongs to the Grand Orient. Therefore, I believe that the Republic should no longer allow any secret societies. I no longer want to have anything to do with the Grand Orient and Masonic meetings."

The Illuminati could not forgive this and for obvious reasons could not allow him on the throne. They exacted their revenge upon him, despite the fact that his vote had been decisive in the process of deposing the king.

Old friends are quick to turn on you once you no longer support the Agenda.

The Terreur was truly a horrific time in the country's history. 300,000 peasants and commoners were executed arbitrarily during that time. It literally decimated the population of 3 million. The influence of the Jacobins' extreme methods was so strong among the World's dictators, that in 1903, Lenin proclaimed, "A Russian social democrat must be a Jacobin".

Quickly after the beginning of the Terror, wars came about for the Nation. On April 20, 1792, war on Austria was declared. Then came Belgium, Holland and finally Germany. Now this is interesting, because as we have established, Weishaupt, the founder of Bavarian Illuminized Masonry and emissary of the Rothschilds, was German. Could the French Revolution have been just a stepping stone to establish the Commune of Mainz? Looking deeper in the matter, we see that the Commune of Mainz was declared on March 18, 1793. That date is particularly significant as on March 18, 1314, Jacques de Molay, the Jewish Grand Master of the Knights Templar, had been burned at the stake. Coincidence?

In the meantime, Louis XVI was still incarcerated following the events of his botched escape attempt in Varennes. Louis was officially arrested on August 13, 1792, and sent to the Temple, an ancient fortress in Paris that was used as a prison. On the 21st of September, the National Assembly declared France to be a Republic and abolished the Monarchy. Louis was stripped of all of his titles and honors, and from this date was known as simply Citoyen Louis Capet.

The leaders of the Commune lobbied for his execution. The legal background of many of the deputies made it difficult for a great number of them to accept an execution without the due process of law of some sort, and it was voted that the deposed monarch be tried before the National Convention, the organ that housed the representatives of the sovereign people.

22

In many ways the former King's trial represented the trial of the Revolution.

The trial was seen as such, with the death of one came the life of the other. Michelet, a prominent French author, argued that the death of the former king would lead to the acceptance of violence as a tool for happiness. He said, "If we accept the proposition that one person can be sacrificed for the happiness of the many, it will soon be demonstrated that two or three or more could also be sacrificed for the happiness of the many. Little by little, we will find reasons for sacrificing the many for the happiness of the many, and we will think it was a bargain." But his argument did not convince the Commune, and they went on with their plans.

He was indicted on grounds of high treason and crimes against the nation. On January 15, 1793, the Convention, composed of 721 deputies, voted on the verdict. Given overwhelming evidence of Louis's collusion with the invaders, the verdict was a foregone conclusion, with 693 deputies voting guilty, none for acquittal, with 23 abstaining. The next day, a roll-call vote was carried out to decide upon the fate of the former King, and the result was uncomfortably close for such a dramatic decision. 288 of the Deputies voted against death and for some other alternative, mainly some means of imprisonment or exile. 72 of the Deputies voted for the death penalty, but subject to a number of delaying conditions and reservations. 361 of the Deputies voted for Louis's immediate death. Philippe Égalité, Louis' own cousin, voted for Louis' execution, a cause of much future bitterness among French monarchists.

The next day, a motion to grant Louis XVI reprieve from the death sentence was voted down: 310 of the Deputies requested mercy, but 380 of the Deputies voted for the immediate execution by the death penalty. This decision would be final. On Monday, the 21st of January 1793, Louis was beheaded by guillotine on the Place de la Révolution.

The executioner, Charles Henri Sanson, testified that the former King had bravely met his fate. Louis indeed declared at death's door that he forgave those who were the cause of his misfortunes. He said he was willing to die and prayed for the French people.

The result of Louis' death was that the "Widow Capet", as the former queen was called after the death of her husband, plunged into deep mourning; she refused to eat or do any exercise. Marie-Antoinette's health rapidly deteriorated in the following months. By this time, she suffered from tuberculosis and possibly even uterine cancer, which caused her to hemorrhage frequently. Despite her condition, the debate as to her fate was the central question of the National Convention after Louis's death. She was finally tried by the Revolutionary Tribunal on October 14, 1793.

Unlike the king, who had been given time to prepare a defense, the queen was given less than one day. Among the things she was accused of (most, if not all, of the accusations were untrue) were orchestrating orgies in Versailles, sending millions of livres of treasury money to Austria, plotting to kill the Duke of Orléans, incest with her son, declaring her son to be the new king of France, and orchestrating the massacre of the Swiss Guards in 1792.

On October 16, 1793, her hair was cut off and she was driven through Paris in an open cart, wearing a plain white dress. At 12:15 PM on October 16, 1793, two and a half weeks before her thirty-eighth birthday, Marie Antoinette was beheaded at the Place de la Révolution. Her last words were, "Pardon me sir, I meant not to do it", to Henri Sanson, her executioner, whose foot she had accidentally stepped on after climbing the scaffold.

In 1793, a band of rebels in Vendée got together under the name of Chouans. They roamed the countryside and gathered forces in the villages they passed. As they gained strength and numbers, the Comité de Salut Public crushed the rebellion in a total bloodshed, killing over 600,000 people during the insurrection. They clearly made an example of the Chouans, and this pretty much calmed down the spirits.

So why depose Louis the XVI, King of France, and start a Revolution? Well, Absolute Monarchy, with its power directly derived from God himself, is a type of government that cannot change, ever. Unless the regime is toppled. And that is exactly what the Illuminati did. Without a bona fide revolution, they could never have achieved their goals.

And what were those goals? For starters, looking at the post-Revolution French society, the government reached a deficit that made the pre-Revolutionary debts seem quite modest in comparison. The debt equaled 800 tons of gold, or 40 per cent of the total gold production of the world during the entire18thcentury. And a society in debt needs money. Of course, the Illuminati, via the Rothschilds in Europe, held the most accessible money supply of the time.

The populace suffered greatly in economical terms as well. With the harassment of churches and anything ecclesiastical, the charity system was annihilated. By the time Napoleon took over power in his coup of 1799, one in five Parisian lived by begging. Of course, a weakened society, a society that is disheartened by years of oppression is a lot easier to manipulate and fool. By 1780 financial paralysis was making its appearance in France. The world's big financiers were firmly established. "They possessed so large a share of the world's gold and silver stocks, that they had most of Europe in their debt, certainly France," writes McNair Wilson in his Life of Napoleon.

Furthermore, the wars brought upon by the Revolution indebted the country further, but also resulted in the Commune of Mainz. With Weishaupt now at the head of the German commune, the Illuminati were one step closer to the New World Order they were thriving for.

The Illuminati wanted to politicize society. Why? Because a divided society is easier to conquer. Remember how in October 1789 they moved the Assembly to an old horse manège, creating the political Left and Right? Suddenly, instead of having a caste system where everyone within one category pretty much agreed with their neighbors, now all citizens were equal but divided.

The few lodges left after the Revolution started preparing for a World Revolution. The idea was to establish a World Power. This was truly, and already, the ultimate goal of the Illuminati.

Unfortunately, the involvement of France and in particular Louis the XVI personally, via his emissary the Marquis de La Fayette, in the Anglo-American war was a problem in establishing that World Power. Indeed, the Illuminati had it all figured out over in the New World, and the Independence War was just a piece of their complicated puzzle. To divert Europe's attention from America, nothing like a domestic quarrel. The Illuminati therefore handcrafted an internal conflict that captivated the interest of all neighboring European Nations.

The Terror was reined in by the assassinations of Danton and DesMoulins by guillotine, the murder of Marat in his bathtub by Charlotte Corday, and the beheading of Robespierre. The very leaders who had instigated the Revolution and put the machine in motion succumbed to their own thirst for power and blood.

On 18 Brumaire 1799 (November 9, 1799), Napoleon Bonaparte (who had francisized his name by then) orchestrated a coup to take over power. Decidedly, he did not act alone and such a coup d'état had to be backed by higher power (guess who?). No soldier, regardless how brilliant a strategist, can ascend to power this fast. Regardless of how he obtained omnipotence for himself, Napoleon was a great ambassador for the Illuminati until he became ruthless and was himself deposed by the very people who had placed him in the highest position imaginable at the time.

Chapter 2: The Assassination of Abraham Lincoln

Abraham Lincoln was the 16th President of the United States. He served from March 1861 to April 1865, when he was assassinated.

Raised on the western frontier of Kentucky, Lincoln was mostly self-taught and became a Prairie Lawyer in Illinois. Throughout the years, he promoted rapid modernization of the economy through banks, canals, railroads and tariffs to encourage the building of factories. After a debate during which he publicly opposed the expansion of slavery, Lincoln lost the Senate race to the Democratic candidate. He thereafter secured the Presidential Nomination for the Republican Party in 1860.

With almost no support in the Southern States, Lincoln won the Northern States and was elected President of the United States in 1860. His election prompted seven southern slave states to form the Confederacy. No compromise or reconciliation was found regarding slavery.

The attack on Fort Sumter on April 12, 1861, is widely regarded as what started the Civil War. Lincoln concentrated his efforts on avoiding war, but when it became evident that war was inevitable, his goal was to reunite the country.

Lincoln made several moves toward ending slavery, centered on the Emancipation Proclamation in 1863, using the Army to protect escaped slaves, encouraging the border-states to outlaw slavery, and helping push through Congress the 13th Amendment to the United States Constitution, which permanently outlawed slavery.

In a statement to Congress in 1865, President Abraham Lincoln states, "I have two great enemies, the Southern Army in front of me, and the financial institutions in the rear. Of the two, the one in my rear is my greatest foe."

On April14, 1965, he was assassinated by John Wilkes Booth at the Ford Theater.

Who was John Wilkes Booth?
John Wilkes Booth was a well-known actor of the time. He also happened to be a staunch Confederate, vocally opposed to Lincoln and his views on the abolition of slavery.

The original plot was to kidnap the President and scare him into changing his policies. However, the plans were changed when on April11, 1865, John Wilkes Booth attended a speech President Lincoln gave promoting voting rights for Blacks. John Wilkes Booth was incensed by this and decided that rather than kidnapping the President, he would assassinate the President.

Did Booth get the idea on his own? Was he financially motivated to switch from a kidnapping to an assassination?

Upon learning that Lincoln and his wife would attend a play at the Ford Theater, he took this opportunity to put his plan into gear.

After the intermission, Lincoln's personal bodyguard left his side to go have a drink with the coachman next door. Coincidence? Lincoln was left vulnerable in his balcony box. Booth crept up and shot him point blank, in the head. Lincoln succumbed to his injuries some nine hours after the attack.

John Wilkes Booth, in the interim, escaped capture at that time and fled. He was on the run for several days before finally being caught on April 26, 1865, on a farm in Virginia. After a brief stand-off with Union Troops, John Wilkes Booth was killed, taking with him to the tomb the real motives behind the assassination.

Was slavery really the only reason the Civil War raged on?

Of course, slavery was not the only reason for the Civil War. But that is not what American Citizens are taught in school. We are told from a young age that the Civil War was essentially a war to end slavery. But in reality, as Otto Von Bismark, Chancellor of Prussia, remarked in 1876, the threat of the United States becoming one strong economic power scared the banking families of the Old World. This had to be stopped. As he said, "The division of the United States into federations of equal force was decided long before the Civil War by the high financial powers of Europe. These bankers were afraid that the US, if they remained as one block, and as one nation, would attain economic and financial independence, which would upset their financial domination over the world."

History reveals that the Rothschilds funded the Civil War. The North was financed by the Rothschilds through their American agent August Belmont and the South was financed through the Erlangers, who were the Rothschilds' relatives. Any which way you look at it, the war was a win-win situation for the Rothschilds.

However, Lincoln through a monkey wrench in their plans by refusing their loans that had exorbitant interest rates ranging from 24% to 36%! He turned to his friend Colonel Dick Taylor of Chicago for advice. Taylor told Lincoln that his problems would be easily resolved by, in essence, creating his own money. He advised Lincoln to push Congress to pass a bill that would authorize the printing of treasury bills, which would have full legal tender status, and pay the soldiers with them and finance his war efforts with them.

The greenback dollar was born from this action. Lincoln said, "The government should create, issue and circulate all the currency and credit needed to satisfy the spending power of the government and the buying power of consumers. ... The privilege of creating and issuing money is not only the supreme prerogative of Government, but it is the Government's greatest creative opportunity. By the adoption of these principles, the long-felt want for a uniform medium will be satisfied. The taxpayers will be saved immense sums of interest, discounts and exchanges. The financing of all public enterprises, the maintenance of stable government and ordered progress, and the conduct of the Treasury will become matters of practical administration. The people can and will be furnished with a currency as safe as their own government. Money will cease to be the master and become the servant of humanity. Democracy will rise superior to the money power."

Lincoln ordered the printing of $450 million greenbacks. This quickly became a problem for the Wall Street money holders. The Illuminati knew it could not be left uncontrolled.

An editorial for the London Times was published that read, "If this mischievous financial policy, which has its origin in North America, shall become underrated down to a fixture, then that Government will furnish its own money without cost. It will pay off debts and be without debt. It will have all the money necessary to carry on its commerce. It will become prosperous without precedent in the history of the World. The brains and wealth of all countries will go to North America. That country must be destroyed or it will destroy every monarchy on the globe."

It was clear the central banking system and the country associated with it would not be left alone. When Lincoln came to a point where he needed more money, the financiers saw to it that he could not be allowed to print more greenbacks. As a result, Lincoln was forced to comply with their wishes and the National Bank Act of 1863 was passed. From now on, no money would be printed in the United States that would not indebt the country further. Salmon P. Chase, Lincoln's former Secretary of the Treasury, after Lincoln's death lamented, "My agency in promoting the passage of the National Banking act (to the benefit of the international bankers), was the greatest financial mistake in my life. It has built up a monopoly which affects every interest in the country."

In the meantime, Lincoln realized that the Czar of Russia was also having issues with the Rothschild holding his country's money supply hostage. Alexander II was indeed resisting the financiers' efforts to establish a central banking system in Russia. Lincoln then unexpectedly got some help from the Tsar who announced that if England or France got involved in the American Civil War, he would take this as a declaration of war, and take President Lincoln's side.

What's a Rothschild to do?

They took one of their own, John D. Rockefeller, and used him to create an oil business in the United States, Standard Oil. With the added funds and their strengthened presence in the US, they decide to back the Democratic candidate in the 1860 presidential election. Much to their sorrow, however, Lincoln won that election.

So why eliminate Lincoln?

He was definitely a threat to the bankers and the people controlling the world funds. If Lincoln saw the end of the Civil War, he would without a doubt pass policies to end the National Bank Act, thus reverting to an America free of debt toward the international bankers. He planned for a Reconstruction policy which would resume agricultural production. However, the Rothschilds and other Illuminati families were content with lower production since it artificially rose the prices, much to their advantage.

What was the solution? Getting rid of the problem. Therefore it was devised to assassinate Lincoln.

Otto von Bismark commented after Lincoln's death, "The death of Lincoln is a disaster for Christendom. There is no man in the United States great enough to wear his boots. I fear those foreign bankers with their craftiness and tortuous tricks will entirely control the exuberant riches of America, and use it systematically to corrupt modern civilization. They will not hesitate to plunge the whole of Christendom into wars and chaos in order that the earth should become their inheritance."

Chapter 3: The Sinking of the Titanic and the Murder of Powerful Individuals Who Opposed the Creation of the Federal Reserve

In 1997, Leonardo DiCaprio shot to international fame when he starred in the James Cameron movie, *Titanic*. For many, this was the opportunity to learn more about the Titanic story, but unfortunately, Hollywood manipulated the story to its standards, omitting most of the truth.

RMS Titanic was a British passenger liner with a total capacity of 2,435 passengers and 892 crew members, for a total of 3,327 people. Ordered in September 1908, to look like her sisters the Olympic and the Britannic, the Titanic was scheduled for her maiden voyage on April 10, 1912 out of Southampton, UK.

Built in Belfast by Harland and Wolff for White Star lines, the Olympic had been finished roughly a year before the Titanic, but had a poor track record. Her first major mishap occurred on her fifth voyage on the 20th of September 1911, when she collided with a British warship, HMS Hawke, off the Isle of Wright. Captain Edward Smith, who later took command of the Titanic, was in command at the time of the accident.

With the Olympic sent back to dock, Harland and Wolff were forced to delay the completion of the Titanic. The Titanic was set to sail for her maiden voyage on April 10, 1912. Delaying that voyage would cost the company money and surely anger passengers who would want refunds. While it was decided that the Olympic would be patched up as fast as possible to leave enough time to work on the Titanic, time was against the promoters and a fast decision had to be made.

This is when J.P. Morgan, the boat's contractor, made the unthinkable decision to switch the Olympic and the Titanic. He figured that since the Olympic could get afloat, he would have more time to finish the Titanic, and would not need to delay the launch.

Captain Smith, a Jesuit (Illuminati sympathizer), agreed to the switch and told J.P. Morgan that he would go with the plan to pretend the Olympic was the Titanic. He had been told that the ship would be purposely sunk at certain coordinates, and that numerous ships would be waiting in the vicinity, thus risking no lives. The result would be collecting insurance money for the "Titanic", some of which would go to Captain Smith himself.

So off they went, and they erased all evidence that the Olympic was the Titanic, switching any and all items that had an individual reference to the ships such as the dinnerware, the linens, and of course the lifeboats.

On April 10, 1912, the "Titanic" was ready to set off for her long-awaited maiden voyage, with 2,228 passengers and crew members on board. The five day transatlantic journey would take the ship from Southampton, UK to New York, USA.

Just past midnight on April 14, 1912, near Canada's Newfoundland, the ship encountered a massive iceberg. Despite having been warned of the dangers of drifting ice in the area, the Captain kept his course to make sure he would be at the right place, at the right time to sink the ship. Unfortunately, this happened too soon, and not exactly as planned. As a result, 1,523 people perished in the sinking of the "Titanic", as the lifeboats on board the ship could only help 1,174 people. The 705 survivors were helped by the RMS Carpathia, ship which took them to New York.

What do the Illuminati have to do with this tragedy?

First of all, the name J.P. Morgan mentioned above should have made you raise an eyebrow. This is the same J.P. Morgan as in the modern day JP Morgan Chase bank. As you'll recall, Chase bank was controlled by the Illuminati family the Rockefellers. J.P. Morgan was a Rothschild agent, a financier and banker from New York. At the height of Morgan's career during the early 1900s, he and his partners had financial investments in many large corporations and were accused by critics of controlling the nation's high finance. He directed the banking coalition that quelled the Panic of 1907, a financial crisis that nearly crippled America by providing "liquidity" to "save" the system. He was the leading financier of the Progressive Era, and his dedication to efficiency and modernization helped transform American business.

Interestingly enough, J.P. Morgan was scheduled to take part in the Titanic's maiden voyage, but pulled out at the last minute, opting to stay on shore instead.

Did he have a premonition? Or did he know what was going to happen?

Let's now take a closer look at an event that, on first view, seems unrelated to the sinking of the Titanic.

In 1907, an engineered economic panic spread across the United States resulting in massive runs on the banks because the depositors were truly concerned and worried about the solvency of these banks. Investors were ruined and things got worse over the next few years. Congress was pressed for a solution and felt that something needed to be done quickly.

In response a small group of men in the positions of power in the government and the banking industry agreed to meet in secret at a place called Jekyll Island to outline a plan for reform. This small group included Senator Nelson Aldrich, Frank Vanderlip of National City (Citibank), Henry Davison of Morgan Bank who was a partner of JP Morgan (a Rothschild agent), and Paul Warburg of the Kuhn, Loeb Investment House who was also an agent of the Rothschilds who was specifically sent to America by them to create a Rothschild controlled Central Bank.

The end result of this secret meeting was the creation of The Federal Reserve. The Federal Reserve Act was passed by Congress in 1913 while most of its members were on Christmas vacation giving all powers to this newly created central bank to issue legal tender and regulate the money supply as it saw fit.

The whole aim and goal of the Illuminati's creation of a Central Bank in America was to bankrupt the country and force the people into economic enslavement which is why the I.R.S. was created in 1914 right after the Federal Reserve Act was passed in 1913. The international bankers needed an agency to collect from the United States citizens the money that was owed to them. The United States government borrows money from the Federal Reserve to run the country and fight wars. When they borrow this money they use the citizens as collateral without them even knowing it. Most people also think that the I.R.S. is a governmental agency, but it is not. It is privately owned and has no organizational or legal ties to the US Treasury Department.

How is this related to the Titanic? Well, some of the richest people in the world opposed the creation of a Federal Reserve Bank. In fact, there were three powerful vocal personalities denigrating the impending creation of the Federal Reserve.

- Benjamin Guggenheim was an American businessman, whose daughter, art collector Marguerite "Peggy" Guggenheim later created the famed eponymous museum.
- Isidor Straus was the head of the already large and famous Macy's Department Stores.
- John Jacob Astor, who was probably the wealthiest man in the world at that time, who had made his fortune mostly in real estate.

The combined fortune of these men was upward of 500 million dollars in 1912. It would be the equivalent of 2 trillion dollars in 2014 dollars. The initiators and proponents of the proposed idea for a Federal Reserve knew that these three powerful financial titans could stall and even stop their efforts to create the Federal Reserve, simply by the sheer amount of money they could freely pour into the economy if they so desired.

By some coincidence (really?), these three men were invited on board the Titanic for her maiden journey and all happily and voluntarily boarded the ship on the morning of April 10, 1912 in Southampton, UK.

All three perished during the fatal events of April 14-15, 1912.

World War I was ignited less than a year later and this war was funded by the Rothschilds and their newly formed Federal Reserve Bank.

One last thing. The lucky survivors of the Titanic were not just sent home to their loving families. It took three days to go from Newfoundland to New York, a trip normally made in less than a day. And once the crew members returned to their native England, they were held for 24 hours in a small shed and sworn to secrecy. Since when do survivors of a tragedy have to be sworn to secrecy, unless someone (the Illuminati?) did not want the word to get out that ship would have, no matter what, been sunk?

Chapter 4: The Assassination of the Archduke Franz Ferdinand

Any textbook recounting the start of World War I will tell you it started on June 28, 1914, when the Archduke Franz Ferdinand was assassinated in Sarajevo, in modern day Bosnia-Herzegovina, by the terrorist group The Black Hand.

But is it really that simple?

First of all, let's take a look at the protagonists in this event. Who was the Archduke Franz Ferdinand?

Franz Ferdinand was an Archduke of Austria-Este, Austro-Hungarian and Royal Prince of Hungary and of Bohemia, and from 1889 until his death, heir presumptive to the Austro-Hungarian throne. He was the nephew of Franz Joseph of Austria.

The Austro-Hungarian royalty was part of the Hapsburg bloodline, which is one of the black nobility bloodlines. In 1889, Franz Ferdinand's cousin, Crown Prince Rudolph, committed suicide, leaving Franz's father, Karl Ludwig, as heir presumptive to the throne of the realm. Almost immediately, Karl Ludwig renounced the throne, de facto making his son, Franz Ferdinand, the new heir presumptive. Karl Ludwig died in 1896 from the typhoid fever, so the fate of Franz Ferdinand would have been inevitable, even if his father had not given up his rights.

Franz Ferdinand acted in a manner that did not show much appreciation for his position. Indeed, he traveled the world and engaged in adventurous activities, such as safaris and round-the-world sailing, putting the future of the Austro-Hungarian succession in danger. This certainly could not have pleased the current monarch, as the succession was already fragile as it was.

Franz Ferdinand was a dreamer and a free-spirit. His military career did not bring him much satisfaction, and then he fell in love which can be a problem for royalty. The Austro-Hungarian long-standing tradition, and therefore law of the land, was that the King (or heir presumptive, for that matter) could only marry someone of royal blood. Franz's love interest, Sophie Chotek, was a commoner. Franz refused to listen to reason and, at the risk of losing the empire, had Pope Leo XIII and Czar Nicholas II of Russia plead to Franz Joseph on his behalf to change the law and allow him to marry Sophie. The disagreement between Franz Joseph and Franz Ferdinand was undermining the stability of the monarchy.

Finally, in 1899, Emperor Franz Joseph agreed to permit Franz Ferdinand to marry Sophie, on condition that the marriage would be morganatic (meaning it would be recognized as a marriage between people of unequal social ranks, which prevents the passage of the husband's titles and privileges to the wife and any children born of the marriage) and that their descendants would not have succession rights to the throne. Sophie would not share her husband's rank, title, precedence, or privileges; as such, she would not normally appear in public beside him. She would not be allowed to ride in the royal carriage or sit in the royal box in theaters. Talk about a compromise!

Yet Franz Ferdinand was so infatuated with Sophie, he agreed to all these terms. And so on July 1, 1900, Franz Ferdinand married Sophie Chotek, leaving his own succession uncertain.

At first, Sophie was called Princess of Hohenberg. In 1909, she gained the title of Duchess of Hohenberg. This raised her status considerably, but she still yielded precedence at court to all the archduchesses. Whenever a function required the couple to assemble with the other members of the imperial family, Sophie was forced to stand far down the line, separated from her husband. You can imagine this was rather awkward.

Politically speaking, Franz Ferdinand had dissenting views from his uncle Franz Joseph. In fact, he was generally more liberal concerning the country's ethnic minorities. He wanted to grant greater autonomy to the Croats, Bosnians and Bohemians (modern-day Czechs). He, however, had nothing but disdain for the Hungarian people, going as far as saying once in 1904, "The Hungarians are all rabble, regardless of whether they are minister or duke, cardinal or burgher, peasant, hussar, domestic servant, or revolutionary." He went as far as treating Hungarian nationalism as a threat to the Hapsburg Dynasty.

His feelings toward the Serbs were similar to those he harbored toward the Hungarian. However, he also recognized that a harsh treatment of the Serbs would inevitably lead to a conflict with Russia, Serbia's ally.

Franz Ferdinand did not necessarily have a lot of supporters among Europe's leaders. He reportedly once described the "dwarf states like Belgium and Portugal" as being inefficient powers on the European political scene. Portugal and Belgium were both part of the traditional Hapsburg Dynasty. The Hapsburg Netherlands, established in 1482, comprised modern-day Belgium, and of course Portugal was an intricate part of the House of Hapsburg. So in essence, Franz Ferdinand blatantly disrespected the Hapsburg ascendancy.

Fast forward to 1914. Gravilo Princip, a 19 year old Bosnian Serb, was a member of Unification or Death, better known as The Black Hand, a Serb Nationalist group created in 1901 and was controlled by the elite advocated for Serbia's independence.

Princip's downfall was his small stature. Seriously.

In 1912, Serbs were being mobilized for the First Balkan War. Princip sought to be accepted in the rebel groups, but was rejected on several occasions due to his frail and weak nature. Vladimir Dedijer, a Serbian politician, later said this continual reminder of Princip's inadequacy was "one of the primary personal motives which pushed him to do something exceptionally brave in order to prove to others that he was their equal".

Constant rejection forced Princip to learn pistol, bomb and knife management practices on his own. He was subsequently accepted within the ranks of The Black Hand for his exceptional skills. The main objective of the Black Hand was the creation, by means of violence, of a "Greater Serbia". Its stated aim was: "To realize the national ideal, the unification of all Serbs. This organization prefers terrorist action to cultural activities; it will therefore remain secret".

In 1913, Archduke Franz Ferdinand had been appointed Inspector General of the Austro-Hungarian Army. In the summer of 1914, General Oskar Potiorek, Governor of the Austrian provinces of Bosnia-Herzegovina, invited the Inspector of the Armed Forces to watch his troops on maneuvers.

So on June 28, 1914, Archduke Franz Ferdinand and Duchess Sophie of Hohenberg headed to Sarajevo. It had been arranged that Franz Ferdinand and Sophia would be taken by car from the train station to City Hall that day. The day of the visit was ill-chosen however, because it was the anniversary of the 1389 Kosovo Polje, or Battle of Kosovo. On this day, the Serbia's Christian Warriors had been defeated by the Turks, and it was regarded as an important holiday. The Serb Nationalists' emotions were therefore running on high on the day of the Archduke's visit.

A majority of the people who lived in Bosnia-Herzegovina despised the Austro-Hungarian rule and wanted a union with Serbia. Many assassination attempts were made against government officials in the past in the attempt to achieve those aims. Franz Ferdinand knew that his life in danger because he had told his friend Count Czerin that he had expected an attempt on his life because he had found out a year before that the Freemasons were plotting to kill him.

Yet, the stubborn presumptive heir did not want to postpone his visit. Upon arriving in Sarajevo on this beautiful summer morning, Franz Ferdinand found flag-waving crowds gathered to greet him. Flowers paved the roads and Franz Ferdinand felt pretty good about his visit. Under all appearances, it looked like the visit would be a complete success.

The six-car motorcade was making its way through the winding Sarajevo streets according to schedule. On the path of the motorcade, The Black Hand had lined up six shooters. The first to see the target was Mehmed Mehmedbasi. He did not take his shot, as he was unable to secure the target. It was up to his eight accomplices to finish the job.

In front of the Central Police Station, Black Hand member Cabrinovic threw a hand grenade at the Ferdinand's car. Franz Ferdinand's driver accelerated and the grenade hit the next car in the motorcade. A dozen onlookers were killed. Cabrinovic had been instructed to immediately after the deed to swallow a cyanide pill that had been given to each would-be assassin. So he popped the pill, and jumped to his death in the nearby Miljacka River. Except he had not counted on the fact that in the summertime, the Miljacka River is only about 10 centimeters, or 4 inches, deep which was definitely not enough to drown an adult man. Thankfully he had swallowed the cyanide pill. Well, sure, except that the pill did not work. So the unlucky lad was dragged to shore by an angry mob and captured by the authorities.

Alarmed by the assassination attempt, Franz Ferdinand's driver sped away. The remaining four shooters, Cvijetko Popovic, Gavrilo Princip, Danilo Ilic, and Trifko Grabez, were unable to fire their guns or hurl their bombs at the Archduke's car as it was going too fast.

Franz Ferdinand, like the royal he was, decided to go on with the day's planned activities. He thus went to City Hall to have breakfast, as scheduled. He then demanded to be taken to the hospital where the onlookers hit by Cabrinovic's grenade were being treated. Though a member of the Archduke's staff suggested this might be dangerous, General Potiorek, who was responsible for the safety of the royal party, replied, "Do you think Sarajevo is full of assassins?" Had he only known…

The route to the hospital was carefully devised to optimize safety and avoid the city center. On the way to the hospital, Franz Ferdinand's driver took a "wrong turn" and took the car directly down Franz Joseph Street. Who makes a wrong turn on a carefully planned route? Unless he had been prompted to do so.

The driver slowed down to the cries of General Potiorek that he had taken the wrong street. With the supposed intent of backing up the car, he conveniently came to a stop.

Gravilo Princip was in a nearby café and jumped at the opportunity to complete the mission. He ran to the car, and when he was no more than five feet away from the car, he fired shots with his pistol. Both Franz Ferdinand and his beloved Sophie were hit, and died shortly thereafter of their fatal gunshot wounds.

Princip forgot to swallow his cyanide pill and was captured. With both Princip and Cabrinovic in custody, they eventually gave in to the skillful interrogation by the authorities and gave up the names of their accomplices.

Mehmed Mehmedbasi escaped to Serbia, but Grabez, Ilic, Cubrilovic, Popovic, and two others, were arrested and charged with treason and murder.

Lucky for Princip, he was 19 at the time of the assassination and since Austro-Hungarian law prohibited anyone under 20 to be sentenced to the capital punishment, he was sentenced to the maximum sentence of 20 years in prison. He died on April 28, 1918 of tuberculosis, six months before the war he had helped start ended. Let's not forget that tuberculosis was a very common cause of death at the time, so common that people would not think twice when told one had died from tuberculosis, and would not even suspect foul play could have been involved.

The unfortunate events of June 28, 1914, led to the start of World War I. The Austro-Hungarian government demanded that the plotters who had escaped, including Mehmed Mehmedbasi, be turned over in the assassination investigation to face trial in Vienna. The Serbs refused. The Prime Minister of Serbia, Nikola Pasic, told the Austro-Hungarian government that he was unable to hand over these three men as it "would be a violation of Serbia's Constitution and criminal law."

The Austro-Hungarian government accused Serbia of murder. They then declared war on Serbia. World War I had begun.

Why get rid of Franz Ferdinand?

Obviously this was the plan all along by the international Illuminati bankers headed by the Rothschilds to bring about World War because this is how they make money by financing all sides in a conflict and charging a huge amount of interest in effect indebting the nations to them. In fact, they really don't care who wins a war as long as they make money. The way they financed World War I was the German Rothschild bankers loaned money to the Germans, the British Rothschild bankers loaned money to the British, and the French Rothschild bankers loaned money to the French.

It was also part of the Rothschild's strategy to bring the US into World War I to ensure that the United States government borrowed from the newly formed Federal Reserve Central bank which they controlled. However, to bring the US into the war they needed to pull a rabbit out of the hat and they did with the sinking of the ship the Lusitania.

The United States Marine ship Lusitania was purposely sent into German-patrolled territory and consequently sunk. This prompted the United States to enter into World War I.

The engagement of the United States into the conflict was coordinated by three organizations: the Council on National Defense, the Navy League and the League to Enforce Peace. A quick look at the members of the various organizations speaks for itself. Bernard Baruch, an emissary of the Rothschilds, was a part of the Council on National Defense. J.P. Morgan, another Rothschild agent was at the head of the Navy League and among the members of the League to Enforce Peace was Elihu Root, J.P. Morgan's lawyer Perry Belmont yet another Rothschild agent and Jacob Schiff of the Rothschild's Kuhn, Loeb, and Co.

On a last note, the Assistant Secretary of the Navy in 1914 was Franklin Delano Roosevelt. That would be the same Franklin Delano Roosevelt who became the 32nd President of the United States in 1933 and until 1945, right before and during World War II. And interestingly enough, before both his stints in power during the two World Wars, he was awarding large Navy contracts to sympathizers to the New World Order cause, ahead of any talks of conflict even being substantiated.

Chapter 5: The Assassination of Patrice Lumumba

To understand who Patrice Lumumba was and the actions that he took and why his stance and actions were considered a threat to the Illuminati's Global Empire you have to have a basic understanding of the history of the African country the Congo. So let's begin with its colonial rule by King Leopold II of Belgium. King Leopold II was born in Brussels and was the son of Leopold I. Leopold II succeeded his father on the throne on December 17, 1865.

In 1870, he set up a private venture to colonize the Congo now known as the Democratic Republic of the Congo. He sent Henry Morton Stanley a British explorer to the Congo to basically establish the King's rule. Many explorers or should I say exploiters tried to colonize the Congo River basin before Henry Morton Stanley and King Leopold. However, due to its harsh tropical climate, disease, and resistance from the black aboriginal people of the land, many European explorers (exploiters) were unsuccessful.

Stanley was able to achieve different results and he forced and tortured the native tribes of the land into signing treaties that granted Leopold everything. He set up military posts and forced out most of the slave traders that occupied the region. He was able to conquer and acquire million acres of African land for Belgium. But the Belgium government and its people didn't want to spend the huge sums of money that it took to manage and maintain this distant colonial venture.

Berlin Conference and the "Congo Free State"

At the Berlin Conference in 1884-1885 which basically was a meeting of European nations and the US to carve out Africa and establish rules amongst themselves on how the resources of Africa were to be exploited, King Leopold was recognized as the owner of the Congo River region and he named it the "Congo

Free State". He immediately began to exploit the land and its people. He instituted a virtual slave labor system where he heinously used the inhabitants to extract the valuable resources of the land such as ivory, rubber, copper, gold, diamonds, and cobalt.

Leopold's Reign of Terror

Leopold ruthlessly and brutally murdered 15 million African people in the process to achieve his aims. He burned down villages, farmland and rain forests. He also held African woman as hostages and cut off people's hands when his extraction of resources quotas weren't met. Women and children were also brutally raped and treated sub-humanly. The African people went hungry as Leopold made a fortune by sectioning off different areas of the Congo and leasing them to European corporations and charging them 50% of the extracted wealth.

Leopold attempted to hide these insidious abuses and the people who visited the Congo during Leopold's reign never mentioned a word about the atrocities that existed. However, word soon got out as various historians and journalists wrote about the horrible conditions in the Congo. As a result there was a public outcry and other European nations put pressure on the Belgium government to do something about Leopold and take control of the Congo. However, the Belgium government had no legal jurisdiction to do so and in order to gain control over the Congo they had to purchase it from Leopold. They renamed it and called it Belgian Congo. They also made annual payments to Leopold as a mark of gratitude.

Anti-Colonial and Pan African Movement

By the 1950's, an anti-colonial and Pan African Movement swept across the African Nation. The desire for independence from the European colonial powers reached a bubbling point. The African people of Congo began to demand independence from Belgium. As pressure mounted, Belgium relented and decided to grant independence on June 30, 1960 to the Democratic Republic of the Congo.

But as soon as they granted this independence they sent in troops to protect Katanga which was a city in the Congo that contained an abundance of natural resources and that the Belgium corporations used as an export hub. The military presence of Belgium was in effect for many years allowing Belgium to continue to exploit and profit from the natural resources of the Congo. So even though they granted Congo its independence, it wasn't truly independent because Belgium controlled it.

The Emergence of Patrice Lumumba

Patrice Lumumba was born on July 2, 1925 in Onalua in the Katakokombe region of the Kasai province of the Belgian Congo. He was raised in a Catholic family and educated in a Protestant mission school. After attending the Protestant mission school Lumumba went to work in Kindu-Port-Empain and became active in a club called the évolués and he began to write essays as well as poems for the Congolese Journals.

He went on to work in Leopodville which was named after King Leopold and is now known as Kinshasa as a postal clerk. He then went to become an accountant at the post office. Lumumba became more politically involved in 1955 when he became regional President of the Congolese trade union of government employees. This union unlike the others was not affiliated with the two Belgian trade unions. Lumumba also became involved with the Belgian Liberal Party where he edited and distributed party literature.

In 1955, after a returning from a trip from Belgium where he was on a study tour, Lumumba was arrested for embezzlement of post office funds. He was sentenced to two years in prison which was reduced to 12 months and he was released in July of 1956. Two years later he along with others founded the

Mouvement National Congolais (MNC) which was the Congolese National Movement and the first nationwide Congolese political party. A couple months later, he attended the first All-African People's Conference (AAPC) that was held in Ghana and featured many black nationalists which included Kwame Nkrumah leader of the newly independent Ghana.

Lumumba was influenced heavily by the ideals and goals of Pan-Africanism which was expressed at the conference and as a result he took on a more militant nationalistic approach. In fact, one of the discussions that took place at this conference was over the legitimacy and desirability of using violence against the colonial powers. It was concluded that violence was necessary in some cases. Some of the signs that were held up at the conference by the people of Ghana contained slogans such as:

- "Down With Imperialism and Colonialism"
- "Africa Must Be Free"
- "We prefer independence with danger to servitude in tranquility"
- "Hands Off Africa"

In December 1959, the Belgian government announced a program that intended to lead the Congo towards independence through proposed local elections. However, this was rejected by the black nationalists of the Congo who viewed this as nothing more than a scheme to install a puppet government before independence. They announced that they were boycotting these elections. As a result they were met with repression by the Belgian government. There was a clash in Stanleyville that resulted in 30 deaths and Patrice Lumumba was charged with inciting a riot and imprisoned. Lumumba was sentenced to 69 months in prison.

The MNC made a tactical move to shift tactics and enter the elections. They won the elections by receiving 90% of the vote.

In January 1960 the Belgian government called a round table conference in Brussels consisting of all Congolese parties to decide the future of the Congo, but the MNC refused to attend without Patrice Lumumba. Lumumba was then released from prison to attend the conference. The conference agreed on the date for independence. That date was June 30, 1960 with elections to be held in May.

Patrice Lumumba the First Prime Minister of the Congo

The MNC won the elections and a right to form a government. They announced Patrice Lumumba as the first Prime Minister of the Congo and Joseph Kasavubu as its President. Independence Day was celebrated on June 30, 1960 and it was attended by Belgian King Baudouin, many dignitaries and the foreign press. .As a sign of things to come King Baudouin's speech ridiculously praised the developments of the Congo under colonialism and his uncle King Leopold II. He also stated the following in his speech:

"Don't compromise the future with hasty reforms, and don't replace the structures that Belgium hands over to you until you are sure you can do better... Don't be afraid to come to us. We will remain by your side, give you advice."

The newly elected President Kasavubu actually thanked the King, but Patrice Lumumba delivered an impromptu speech that reminded the audience that the independence of the Congo wasn't granted generously or without struggle. He said the following:

"For this independence of the Congo, even as it is celebrated today with Belgium, a friendly country with whom we deal as equal to equal, no Congolese worthy of the name will ever be able to forget that it was by fighting that it has been won, a day-to-day fight, an ardent and idealistic fight, a fight in which we were spared neither privation nor suffering, and for which we gave our strength and our blood. We are proud of this struggle, of tears, of fire, and of blood, to the depths of our being, for it was a noble and just struggle, and indispensable to put an end to the humiliating slavery which was imposed upon us by force".

This speech became a media sensation in the West and Western powers saw Lumumba as a serious threat because he was a revolutionary who wanted the Congolese people as well as the African people worldwide to see themselves as equals with their former colonizers & enslavers, a view that basically sealed his fate.

There was dissent within the army only a few days after independence. General Janssens, an army head, told the soldiers that their lot would not change much after independence so the soldiers rebelled in protest. Moise Tshombe who was from the powerful ethnic group Lunda and backed by the Belgian mining monopoly Union Minière du Haut Katanga took advantage of the chaos and used it as an opportunity to claim that the mineral rich province of Katanga was seceding from the Congo.

He was ordered to do this by the Belgian government who never had any real intentions of giving up their control of the Congo and the wealth that Katanga generated. Katanga was the source for the bulk of Congo's copper, cobalt, uranium, gold and other natural resources. The Belgians sent in troops and the United States President Dwight Eisenhowser supported the Belgian military intervention on behalf of Katanga. He did this mainly because he saw Lumumba's ideology as a threat to the Western colonial imperialist powers and many prominent US officials and US corporations had financial ties to Katanga's wealth.

Belgian's intervention was denounced by the Soviet Union and many other countries. This led the United Nation Security Council to authorize the withdrawal of Belgian troops and have them replaced by a United Nations military force. The United

Nations military force intervened in Katanga, but it did not end the secession. Unable to stop the revolt Lumumba appealed to the United Nations and the United States for help, but he was refused so he turned to the Soviet Union and they assisted him with food, medical supplies, trucks and planes to transport his troops to Katanga.

On September 5, 1960 President Kasavubu a CIA stooge dismissed Lumumba as Prime Minister. Lumumba questioned the legality of the dismissal. Lumumba tried to broadcast his position on the radio to the Congolese people however, the UN military force shut down the radio station. Meanwhile President Eisenhowser according to findings by the Senate Select Committee which said there was "reasonable inference" to believe the following assertion: that Eisenhowser ordered the assassination of Patrice Lumumba

In fact, the United States role was documented by the 1975 Senate Select Committee on Intelligence hearings which was chaired by Idaho Senator Frank Church. The Senate Select Committee also went on record with the conclusion that CIA Director Allen Dulles had ordered Lumumba's assassination as "an urgent and prime objective" which was Dulles own words. In one of the attempts on Lumumba, a CIA scientist was sent to the Congo with a lethal biological virus that was to be used to assassinate Lumumba. However, that plot was never carried out, because they weren't able to come up with "a secure enough agent with the right access".

On September 14, 1960 Joseph Mobutu (later known as Mobutu Sese Seko) organized a CIA and Belgian sponsored coup and deposed of Prime Minister Lumumba. Lumumba was then placed under house arrest even though UN troops were there supposedly to protect him.

Lumumba "escaped" at night and went to Stanleyville where his supporters had control. I put the word "escaped" in quotes because according to author Karl Evannz this was all a CIA setup. The plan was to lure Lumumba to Stanleyville. According to the author, in a cable to CIA headquarters dated November 14 "Lumumba's escape had been arranged". Lumumba was told by a representative of the UN that his "young daughter was on her deathbed." Lumumba noticed that the house was lightly guarded and desperate to see his dying daughter he escaped. He was captured in Port Francqui by troops that were loyal to Mobutu who knew that he was coming with two of his top aides Joseph Okito and Maurice Mpolo.

The Soviet Union immediately demanded Lumumba's release and called upon the U.N. Security Council to act. However, the Soviet Union resolution was defeated in an 8-2 vote. Mobuto transferred Lumumba over to the Katanga Province and into the hands of Moise Tshombe and he was assassinated along with Okito and Mpolo.

Chapter 6: The Assassination of John F. Kennedy, Robert Kennedy and John F. Kennedy Jr.

John Fitzgerald Kennedy (May 29, 1917 – November 22, 1963), commonly known as "Jack" or by his initials JFK, was the 35th President of the United States.

Like many Kennedys in the United States, JFK was of Irish decent. JFK's bloodline, however, was more noble than most. It can be retraced to the early 11th century Irish king Brian Bóruma mac Cennétig, also known as Brian Boru or Brian Caennedi. His descendants, the Kings of Ormond, formed the O'Kennedy clan. The Kennedys' castles in Ireland were all located near Nenagh in North Tipperary, in the province of Munster. In the early 17th century, the clan settled the Ulster region of Ireland, across the waterway from the Gallaway region of Scotland. As the Scots and the Irish mingled, the bloodline mixed and became one.

The Kennedys of Scotland engendered many prominent figures in the Freemasonry circles.

Starting in the early 16th century with David, 3rd Lord of Kennedy, the Maybole (South Ayrshire, Scotland) dynasty of the Earls of Cassillis was founded. One notable descendant was Archibald Kennedy, 15th Earl of Cassillis (1872-1943). Also known as the Marquess of Ailsa, he was inducted Grand Principle of the Grand Lodge of Scottish Freemasonry in 1913. A key member in the Holywood House Lodge #44 in Edinburgh, Scotland, Archibald had close ties with the British Royal Family.

Fast forward to the 18th century, and the name Matthew Kennedy (1652 -1731) starts emerging as a prominent Illuminati member. After moving from Ireland to Paris, France, Matthew makes the acquaintance of Saint Germain, an Illuminati frontman who, at the time, presided the Illuminati Lodge at Ermenonville, in the Picardie region, northwest of Paris. This illuminated lodge was known for its gruesome blood rituals carried on an altar made of human bones. St. Germain was in part responsible for spreading the Scottish Rite of Freemasonry into France and later Europe, as the movement grew.

It must be noted that Matthew Kennedy evolved in St. Germain's court, and was commandeered to write a genealogy of the Royal Family of the Stuarts of England. Interestingly, the Stuarts had married into the Sang Reel (sangraal – saint grail – Holy Grail), reinforcing the Kennedys' bond to the Illuminati.

The Kennedy bloodline is one of the 13 Illuminati bloodlines. Another prominent Illuminati bloodline is the Auchincloss. Unsurprisingly, JFK is related to the Auchincloss by marriage. His wife, Jacqueline Bouvier, is tied to the Auchincloss through the marriage of Jackie's sister into the clan. Families such as the Rockefellers, Vanderbilts, Winthrops, Grosvernors, Bundys are all results of the Auchincloss bloodline. The co-founders of Standard Oil, John D. Rockefeller and Oliver B. Jennings, are both also related to the ancient Scottish bloodline. It has been told of the relationship of John F. Kennedy, his wife Jacqueline Bouvier and his sister-in-law Caroline Bouvier that they were like step-children to Hugh Auchincloss.

On yet another level, the Kennedys are tied to the Dukes of Devonshire, commonly known as one of the most important Freemason families of England. This connection was sealed via the marriage of Jackie Bouvier and John F. Kennedy.

These connections make it easy to see how the union of the Kennedys and the Bouviers has been reported as an arranged marriage to tighten the relationship between the New World Brotherhood and the Old World Brotherhood. The importance of their coming together was symbolized when Theodore White wrote in a December 1963 article for Life Magazine that their reign was to be likened to Camelot.

In light of his strong bloodline ties to the Illuminati, the ascension to power of John F. Kennedy was facilitated by his own father, Joseph Kennedy, who was a bootlegger during the Prohibition. The Kennedy fortune was mostly amassed when Joseph partnered with "The Prime Minister", Frank Costello, an Italian-American crime boss and mafia gangster. As leader of the Luciano crime family, Costello helped Joseph Kennedy rig the West Virginia and Chicago primaries in 1960, thus securing his son John would win the presidential suffrage. This claim has been substantiated by hard evidence, such as the wire-tapped conversation the FBI intercepted on Chicago crime boss Sam Giancana's phone, during which he admitted to having made a deal with the Kennedys to skew the election results in exchange of immunity from deportation for certain mobsters.

For three years, John F. Kennedy enjoyed a relatively quiet presidency, with no major roadblocks. With Lyndon Baines. Johnson (LBJ) as a supposedly loyal Vice-President, JFK grew complacent.

The turn of events in November 1963 would prove dreadful.

Lee Harvey Oswald

Everyone is familiar with the names Lee Harvey Oswald. Oswald has been portrayed as the President's executor while Ruby assassinated Oswald shortly thereafter. But was he really acting alone, as the public has been fed for 50 years?

To better understand the true connection between Oswald and the Illuminati, we need to establish some important facts.

Lee Harvey Oswald was a US Marine in the years preceding his involvement with the Kennedy assassination. He worked as a radar operator at bases designed for the famous U-2 spy planes. Following his stint in the Marines, Oswald immigrated to Russia where he met and married the niece of a prominent KGB colonel. While in Russia, Oswald sold military secrets related to the U-2 planes in exchange for what was a comfortable lifestyle in the late 1950s communist Russia. In reality, Oswald was a double agent working closely with the CIA and feeding Russian intelligence outdated information.

Upon his return on US soil in 1962, Oswald moved to New Orleans, Louisiana where he became a neighbor of William Guy Banister, a career employee of the FBI and a private investigator. He was also a former Assistant Superintendent of the New Orleans Police Department and had ties with the CIA. Banister was an outspoken defender of the anti-communist movement. Curiously, he befriended Oswald, who was on the opposite end of the spectrum. Oswald was a key player in the Fair Play for Cuba Committee (FPCC), which opposed the efforts of the United States to crush the Cuban opposition. In particular, Oswald was against the 1961 Bay of Pigs invasion and the general embargo on Fidel Castro's Cuba.

In September 1963, Banister's own daughter reported seeing her father's CIA boss interacting in secrecy with Lee Harvey Oswald, when one would have thought that they could not be further from having anything in common. Leaflets for the FPCC, stamped with the address 544 Camp Street, which was Banister's address, were being passed around New Orleans by Lee Oswald himself in late 1962.

John Alex McCone, CIA Director, admitted in a document sent to the FBI, the White House and the State Department on November 26, 1963, that on September 18, 1963, Lee Harvey Oswald was given $6,500 to eliminate a prominent political figure.

It was reported by Dallas Deputy Sheriff Allen Sweatt that Oswald was being paid $200 per month ($1533 in 2014 dollars) by the government and was the proud owner of CIA informant identification number 110669. Oswald also had an FBI informant number attached to his file.

In October 1963, Oswald moved to Dallas, Texas. He rapidly obtained a job at the Texas Book Depository, making $1.25 per hour ($9.58 in 2014 dollars) boxing and shipping books.

How could a simple American citizen, once thought to have defected from the Army and to have committed treason against the United States by selling military secrets, how could such a plain person find himself at the right place, at the right time, all the time? Why would Lee Harvey Oswald have informant numbers, and be on government payroll unless he was doing someone else's bidding?

Lyndon Baines Johnson

Lyndon Baines Johnson was Kennedy's Vice-President. All appearances led to believe that Johnson was in good terms with the President of the United States. His mistress Madeleine Duncan Brown told a different story.

Brown reports that on November 21, 1963, the night before the Assassination, LBJ met with several Dallas Tycoon, political figures, mobsters and FBI moguls at a lodge outside of Dallas.

Among the guests:

- J. Edgar Hoover, first Director of the FBI from 1935 to 1972;
- Richard Nixon, 37th President of the United States, from 1968 to 1974 when Watergate forced him out of office;
- Clyde Tolson, Associate Director of the FBI from 1930 to 1972;
- John J. McCloy, Wall Street lawyer and banker, Assistant Secretary of War during World War II, President of the World Bank and Chairman of Chase Manhattan bank;
- Haroldson Hunt, oil tycoon named one of the 8 richest people of 1952 by Fortune Magazine;

- and Jack Ruby, known as the "in-man" in Texas who could arrange call girls, find drugs, fix gambling issues and contract murders.

Emerging from this meeting of the titans, an irked Johnson reportedly told his beloved Madeleine Brown, "After tomorrow, those SOBs (the Kennedys) will never embarrass me again. That's not a threat. It's a promise."

The appearances on the afternoon of November 22, 1963 were certainly against Lyndon B. Johnson. He was seen ducking in his car, which was part of the Presidential motorcade, 30 to 40 seconds prior to the first shot ringing. Before turning the corner from Main Street to Houston Street, Johnson showed signs of nervousness, as if he anticipated some drastic actions to be taken any moment

To further the rumors of his implication in the assassination, Johnson was seen smiling and winking at Congressman Albert Thomas (D-Houston- 8th District) during his swear-in ceremony mere hours after Kennedy was killed, in blatant view of JFK's widow, Jackie Bouvier Kennedy. Unless he had something to celebrate, such a display of confidence would have been highly inappropriate. Was LBJ so affected by JFK's murder that he had a lapse in judgment? Or was he finally where he wanted to be?

The events of November 22, 1963

President John F. Kennedy was in Dallas on November 22, 1963 to enjoy a luncheon with local businessmen and political figures in preparation for the 1964 presidential election.

His route had been carefully planned and reviewed by the Secret service and was to take him through Downtown Dallas. The 10-mile trip from Dallas Love Field airport had been selected to meander at a slow pace, allowing for maximum public exposure. In the car with President Kennedy were his wife Jackie Bouvier Kennedy, Texas Governor John Connally and the governor's wife Nellie.

The scheduled route was to take the motorcade to Trade Mart on Dealey Plaza at exactly 12:15 PM Central Time. The presidential delegation was running late. Everything seemed quiet and the lovely morning was conducive of a festive mood in the presidential car.

This was about to change drastically.

At 12:29 PM, Nellie Connally, proud to exhibit Texas' warm welcome, turned to the President who was riding in the back and with a smile told him, "Mr. President, you can't say Dallas doesn't love you!" Jack Kennedy was flattered by the remark and acquiesced with a smile.

As he waved to the crowd, his wife at his side, the limousine turned the corner of Elm Street and slowly drove past the Texas Book Depository. The first shot resonated shortly thereafter. Most witnesses did not even react to this first shot, thinking it may simply have been a car backfiring, or a firecracker. Quickly, two more shots followed. Governor Connally panicked and as he tried turning around to see John F. Kennedy, he screamed, "They're going to kill us all!"

The President was shot in the head and, as a result of the impact, immediately lost over 50% of his brain mass, thus killing him on impact. The same bullet then touched Governor Connally in the shoulder. The official line is that three shots were fired. However, about 20% of witnesses have reported a fourth shot coming from the grassy knoll on Elm Street. One thing is for sure, a second shot hit the President.

Chaos ensued and the scene was gruesome. The President's blood and fragments of his scalp, brain, and skull landed on the inside of the car, the inside and outside of the windshield and sun visors, the front engine hood, the rear trunk lid, the Secret Service car behind the presidential car, and its driver's left arm, and officers riding on motorcycles on both sides of the President behind him.

Mrs. Kennedy climbed onto the back of the limousine then was thrust back inside by Secret Service agents. As she told her husband she loved him, she held his skull down to limit brain loss. Unfortunately, her efforts were in vain and the assassination attempt was successful.

Shortly thereafter, as police scurried in the area, trying to find the shooter (or shooters), Lee Harvey Oswald was arrested in the Texas Book Depository where he had been at work.

The timeline inside the book depository is sketchy at best and while it was established to incriminate Oswald, it does little to prove his guilt.

Texas Book Depository secretary Carolyn Arnold testified that she saw Lee Harvey Oswald in the break-room located on the second floor at 12:15 PM. It must be noted that originally, the motorcade was supposed to have arrived at Dealey Plaza at 12:15 PM but was running late. If indeed it had been on time, how could Oswald have the opportunity to set up his gear and carry on the execution?

Back to the timeline as it was officially uncovered, the secretary said she saw Oswald quietly enjoying a Coke, and said she recognized him without a doubt. At 12:20 PM, Bonnie Ray Williams was on the sixth floor, where the shots supposedly originated from, and saw no one around him, and certainly not Oswald. However, interestingly enough, a witness on the ground (Arnold Rowland) said he saw two figures in the sixth floor window that was later designated as the source of the shots. This was shortly past 12:20 PM.

As Oswald was still in the lunchroom, at 12:31 PM, a mere 90 seconds after the President was shot, an out-of-breath patrolman, Marrion Baker, stormed into the snack room and looked around. There stood Oswald and his boss. The officer asked Oswald's boss, "Do you know this man? Does he work here?" The boss said indeed Oswald worked there and the officer, satisfied with this answer, ran out the room, shouting that the President had just been shot. According the Oswald's boss, his reaction was one of someone who hears news for the first time, as he acted surprised and numb.

According to the official timeline, Oswald was a master marksman, who worked at an incredible speed, and seemingly had the ability to be in two places at once. After firing three shots, neatly aligning the shells on one side of the room while wiping all fingerprints off his rifle which he stashed at the opposite side of the room, Oswald ran down four flights of stairs to get back to the lunchroom, where he calmly enjoyed a Coke, never once appearing out of breath. And let's not omit the fact that he would have had to sprint by Victoria Adams and Sandra Styles, who both worked on the second floor near the lunchroom, but who never saw him.

At 1:14 PM, Officer J.D. Tippit was found dead on the street and Lee Harvey Oswald was arrested in conjunction with his murder. He was almost immediately accused of assassinating the President, despite loudly refuting all accusations and claiming he had never shot anyone.

On November 24, 1963, as he was being transferred from the police headquarters to a county jail, Jack Ruby supposedly took justice into his own hands and gunned down Lee Harvey Oswald, silencing forever the only person who could have made sense of the Texas Book Depository incidents.

Of course, this was the same Jack Ruby who, three days earlier on November 21, 1963, had been seen partying with Lyndon B. Johnson and his acolytes.

It must also be noted that Jack Ruby had been identified as one of the figures in the famous Phillip Willis pictures taken directly following the President's assassination. In one of the shots, a man who, as Willis pointed out, "looked so much like Jack Ruby, it's pitiful," could be seen near the entrance of the Texas Book Depository.

Coincidence?

So who was Jack Ruby? Officially, he was a prominent Dallas business man, well known on the nightclub scene. He supposedly shot Lee Harvey Oswald at point-blank range to avenge the death of President Kennedy. They had, however, never been linked before these events.

After being arrested for the execution of Oswald, Jack Ruby used his one phone call to get in touch with Al Gruber. Gruber was a close friend of Mickey Cohen, who just happened to be gangster Meyer Lansky's right-hand man. Cohen had facilitated the relationship between JFK and movie star Marilyn Monroe, whose life ended tragically in August 1962.

Another coincidence?

In an interesting turn of events, Gruber just happened to have come to visit Ruby in Dallas in the days preceding the assassination, and had rekindled his friendship with Ruby, a man he had not had contact with in over a decade.

Jack Ruby was not unfamiliar with the Mafia underground world. He worked with Chicago gangster Al Capone for years, and later Meyer Lansky. Of course, Ruby's connection to Lansky led him to have ties with the CIA.

Let's establish that connection. Lansky was known as the Mob's Accountant. He had developed a gambling empire to include casinos in Las Vegas, the Bahamas, London and Cuba. Along with his partner Lucky Luciano, Lansky created the National Crime Syndicate of the United States. Lansky's ties to the CIA were simple: he was called upon to help oust Castro in 1961 since he had a presence in Cuba via his casinos there.

Lansky later started employing Jack Ruby to do his dirty work and Ruby happily complied.

According to Marita Lopez, a former CIA operative, the day before the Kennedy assassination, she met in Dallas with several key CIA members, including E. Howard Hunt (one of the Three Tramps described below, who later was caught in the Nixon's Watergate scandal) and Jack Ruby. While she was not told what the highly secretive mission would be, Lopez was told that her role would be to be a decoy for the operation. Lopez declined the mission, but recalled the events in a libel hearing opposing E. Howard Hunt and newspaper *The Spotlight.*

Jack Ruby was eventually tried, convicted and sentenced to death. He vowed to reveal some important information about Kennedy's death at his trial hearing. He even asked Chief Justice Earl Warren to transfer him from Dallas to Washington DC for the sake of his personal safety. The request was denied, and Jack Ruby conveniently died in his cell on January 3, 1967, allegedly from a pulmonary embolism due to complications of lung cancer.

Did Ruby's health really deteriorate? Or was he "helped"?

The Three Tramps

Directly following the murder, police forces canvassed the area in the hopes of finding who had executed the President.

The grassy knoll in front of the Texas Book Depository was a recurring theme in witness' accounts of the events. About 20% of the people present at that tragic moment reported hearing a fourth shot coming out of the grassy knoll.

Law enforcement agents rapidly arrested three tramps in a nearby boxcar, despite not fitting the profile of master executioners. The tramps were a man named Raoul, E. Howard Hunt (CIA Officer from 1949 to 1970) and Frank Sturgis. Where things get sketchy is that despite being arrested for one of the highest profile crime in history, these three men were never booked, fingerprinted or photographed. The only photographic evidence is in the pictures several reporters on the scene took when the men were escorted from the railroad to the police cars that took them away, never to be heard from again.

At least not in conjunction with Kennedy's murder.

Indeed, nine years later, in 1972, Frank Sturgis and E. Howard Hunt were arrested during that little scandal known as Watergate. The Nixon burglars, who both worked for the CIA, looked incredibly alike to two of the "tramps" who had been briefly paraded after the Kennedy murder.

The third "tramp," Raoul, was a dead-on doppelganger to a man also named Raoul whose picture circulated widely as being the commandeer of Martin Luther King Jr.'s assassination. The "official" murderer of MLK, James Earl Ray, also admitted to have been set up by a man named Raoul.

Why were these three men, despite evidence they were present during the shooting, set free without further investigation? How could they possibly be linked to yet another major historical milestone in the United States' history nearly a decade after being linked to the President's assassination?

Abraham Zapruder's Movie

As part of the investigation, moments after the President was shot, all still film and live action cameras were confiscated by the public authorities.

All except Abraham Zapruder's movie. Zapruder was a Dallas clothing manufacturer, there to enjoy a glimpse of the presidential motorcade with his family, when he realized that he had taken on film a historical event. He saw an opportunity to take advantage of being the sole owner of such a film and sold it to Time Magazine. Unfortunately, Time Magazine altered several frames of the movie thus compromising the evidence.

Was this done intentionally to cover up the conspiracy? Why would they alter the film knowing that a crime was committed? The bottom line is there were many powerful people behind the scenes who did not want the truth to come out by viewing this film in its original state, which could be the reason why it was tampered with.

The Zapruder movie later played an important role in the Warren Commission, to be discussed further below.

In the meantime, one could wonder what happened to the dozens of films and pictures taken by regular folks that day. Special FBI Agent Regis Kennedy was in charge of gathering those. None of them were ever seen or viewed again.

The House Select Committee on the assassination subpoenaed Regis Kennedy so he could testify as to what may have happened to all these pieces of evidence. Sadly, Special Agent Kennedy was found murdered on the very day he was set to testify. It will then come to no surprise that over 200 witnesses in relation to the JFK Assassination Investigation have disappeared under mysterious conditions, been murdered or have "died of natural causes."

The Warren Commission

Johnson was sworn in as President on Air Force Once at Dallas Love Field in Dallas on November 22, 1963, two hours and eight minutes after JFK was murdered.

On November 29, 1963, a federal investigation was launched at the orders of LBJ. The investigation into JFK's assassination was called the Warren Commission as it was chaired by Supreme Court Chief Justice Earl Warren.

The Warren Commission was composed of seven individuals:

- Chief Justice Earl Warren, a 33rd degree Freemason and rumored to be under the control of the Mafia;

- Allen Dulles, head of the CIA fired by Kennedy, close to the Nazi interests which his law firm defended, and a member of the Illuminati outfits Council on Foreign Relations and the Bilderberg Group (an annual private conference of approximately 120 to 140 invited guests from North America and Europe, most of whom are people of influence);
- John J. McCloy, chairman of the Council on Foreign Relations at the time of JFK's assassination, chairman of the Ford Foundation and chairman of Rockefeller's Chase Manhattan Bank- incidentally, John J. McCloy was also present at Lyndon B. Johnson's get-together outside of Dallas on the evening of November 21, 1963;
- Gerald Ford, 33rd degree Freemason, member of the Illuminati created Council on Foreign Relations and the Bilderberg Group; Nixon's Vice-President; 38th President of the United States (1974-1977);
- Hale Boggs, United States Representative (D-Lousiana), elected in 1946, and subsequently re-elected 13 times until 1972, when his plane mysteriously disappeared during a campaign trip in Alaska;
- John Sherman Cooper, US Senator (R-Kentucky), former judge and US Ambassador to India, served in the Senate from 1952 to 1973, with a hiatus in 1956, then named US Ambassador to the German Democratic Republic from 1974 to 1976;
- J. Lee Rankin, General Counsel appointed to the Justice Department in 1953.

Unofficially, J. Edgar Hoover presented the theory of the "Single Shooter" in which he instilled as common knowledge that Lee Harvey Oswald acted on his own and alone. J. Edgar Hoover was also a 33rd degree Freemason and the Director of the FBI. It would be an understatement to say that John F. Kennedy and

J. Edgar Hoover were far from being associates. As a matter of fact, Kennedy had planned on replacing Hoover as head of the FBI as soon as he was re-elected in 1964.

To better understand the implications of the members of the Warren Commission with the Freemasons and the Illuminati Movement, it is important to define what a 33rd degree Freemason is.

The most common Freemason rite in the United States is the Ancient (and) Accepted Scottish Rite of Freemasonry, trivially called the Scottish Rite, and represented by the double headed eagle, as opposed to the United States single headed eagle. A Freemason Rite is a series of degrees all under the Supreme Council of that particular rite. Each rite is considered sovereign unto itself in the United States. The 33rd degree is the highest attainable degree, one that makes the title's owner a Knight Commander of the Court of Honor and an Inspector General, the highest possible rank in the Scottish Rite. The elite that are allowed the title can only be nominated by peers and must prove major contribution to society. As you can see, the 33rd degree title is reserved to a select few evolving in certain higher circles, all with ties to one another.

The Warren Commission, with its 33rd degree Freemasons and sympathizers, declared in its 888-page final report that Lee Harvey Oswald acted alone and for himself.

The case was closed. But was it truly resolved?

Why Would the Illuminati Want Kennedy Dead?

In any major crime investigation, there are two questions that come to mind, "Who did it," and "Who benefits from the crime."While these two questions are generally related, in the case of John F. Kennedy's assassination, they should be taken separately.

The Warren Commission established that Lee Harvey Oswald did it. That covers the first question. However, no one has ever been able to explain how Oswald could have benefitted from the murder of the United States President. Therefore the question, "Who benefitted," is a valid question in this case. The answer is quite startling.

Lyndon B. Johnson evidently benefitted from the President's murder as he was placed in a position of power within two hours of the murder. In addition to his personal gain, Lyndon Johnson was connected with crime syndicate boss Meyer Lansky and was taking bribes from his crime syndicate in return for granting Lanksy and his syndicate political favors.

Looking back in chronological order, the events leading to the fatal afternoon of November 1963 set up the inevitable denouement to Kennedy's story.

Starting in 1961and more precisely in April, with the invasion of the Bay of Pigs in Cuba. US Forces were trying to overthrow a military coup d'état led by left-wing revolutionary Fidel Castro. The invasion was a debacle and the CIA-supplied troops were captured and interrogated, thus reinforcing Castro's ascension to power. The botched operation led to Kennedy firing Allen Dulles, the then-Director of the CIA. If you'll recall, Dulles was later appointed to the Warren Commission.

In 1962, the Joint Chiefs of Staff presented President Kennedy with what they called Operation Northwoods. In the heart of the Cold War era, and in the light of the rise of Marxist strongholds, such as Cuba, the idea of Operation Northwoods was to inflict terrorist attacks on United States Citizens, and blame them on the enemy. This would be the base to justify wars, political assassinations and various invasions. On a side note, the Council on Foreign Relations an Illuminati organization preaches the benefits of a one-world government, eliminating all opposing the ideology. Kennedy rejected the idea in block. He was outraged that he could be offered the possibility to murder in cold-blood his fellow Americans. This led him to talk about drastic changes, including limiting the CIA's ability to pursue covert operations, and eventually dismantling the CIA. He said he would, "Splinter the CIA in a thousand pieces."

Adding insult to injury, after the firing of Allen Dulles, the idea started germinating that President Kennedy was no longer an asset but a threat to the Illuminati and the development of the New World Order.

On June 4, 1963, John Kennedy took one step further in the direction of his demise. He signed the Executive Order 11110, commonly known as the United States notes order. The ultimate plan was to abolish the Federal Reserve system, and prevent it from printing money backed by foreign interests and making the United States a debtor to the international banking system. Executive Order 11110 was put into effect and money was being printed with the words, "United States Note." minted across the top where the words, "Federal Reserve Note," traditionally were printed. Over $4,000,000 worth of bills were placed into circulation between June 1963 and November 1963.

Eliminating the Federal Reserve was counter-efficient to the interests of the Illuminati banking cartel headed by families like the Rothschilds and the Rockefellers. Also, a self-sufficient United States that controlled its' own money supply would be more prone to resisting the New World Order.

On November 23, 1963, the day after Kennedy's assassination, all of the United States Notes were recalled and taken from circulation, making them nothing more than a pricey collector's item.

The final affront came when on October 11, 1963. Kennedy finalized the National Security Memorandum # 263. This memorandum was prepared to send all troops home from Vietnam. The first wave of 1,000 soldiers was to come home by December 25, 1963, and the United States was to be fully out of

Vietnam by 1965. Secretary of Defense Robert McNamara has been quoted as saying that Kennedy had planned to fully withdraw from Vietnam after the 1964 suffrage. Lyndon B. Johnson was not in agreement with President Kennedy on this matter, adding to the already wide riff between the two men.

Withdrawing from Vietnam would mean allowing communism to prevail in Southeast Asia. In addition the military industrial complex would have lost out on the enormous amounts of profits that it was making from the war.

The day after Kennedy's funeral, on November 26, 1963, LBJ signed National Security Resolution # 273, which abolished National Security Memorandum # 263. Suspiciously, Johnson signed the Gulf of Tonkin Resolution. It authorized the use of military force in Vietnam, without a formal declaration of war. This amounted to an escalation of an already precarious situation in Southeast Asia, leading to more war manufacturing, an industry widely controlled by the mafia.

Although Kennedy never mentioned the name Illuminati in public he did give a speech detesting the secret societies that had tremendous power and influence over domestic and world affairs. He said the following:

"The very word 'secrecy' is repugnant in a free and open society; and we are as a people inherently and historically opposed to secret societies, to secret oaths and to secret proceedings. We decided long ago that the dangers of excessive and unwarranted concealment of pertinent facts far outweighed the dangers which are cited to justify it. Even today, there is little value in opposing the threat of a closed society by imitating its arbitrary restrictions. Even today, there is little value in insuring the survival of our nation if our traditions do not survive with it. And there is very grave danger that an announced need for increased security will be seized upon by those anxious to expand its meaning to the very limits of official censorship and concealment. That I do not intend to permit to the extent that it is in my control. And no official of my Administration, whether his rank is high or low, civilian or military, should interpret my words here tonight as an excuse to censor the news, to stifle dissent, to cover up our mistakes or to withhold from the press and the public the facts they deserve to know".

Then he went on to further state in the same speech:

"For we are opposed around the world by a monolithic and ruthless conspiracy that relies primarily on covert means for expanding its sphere of influence — on infiltration instead of invasion, on subversion instead of elections, on intimidation instead of free choice, on guerrillas by night instead of armies by day. It is a system which has conscripted vast human and material resources into the building of a tightly knit, highly efficient machine that combines military, diplomatic, intelligence, economic, scientific and political operations. Its preparations are concealed, not published. Its mistakes are buried, not headlined. Its dissenters are silenced, not praised. No expenditure is questioned, no rumor is printed, no secret is revealed. It conducts the Cold War, in short, with a war-time discipline no democracy would ever hope or wish to match".

John F. Kennedy was assassinated plain and simple because he went against his own Illuminati brethren.

The Kennedy "Curse"

The Assassination of Robert "Bobby" F. Kennedy

Robert "Bobby" Kennedy was John F. Kennedy's younger brother. At the time of his brother's assassination in 1963, Bobby was a US Attorney General. He had gained fame in1957-1959 as the head of the Labor Rackets Committee established by the Senate. During that time, he publicly challenged Teamsters President Jimmy Hoffa and criticized the corrupt practices of the Unions. Bobby Kennedy even published *The Enemy Within*, a book about corruption in organized labor.

As US Attorney General, Bobby Kennedy also challenged mob boss Meyer Lansky.

In 1964, Bobby Kennedy left his position as a White House advisor and Attorney General to run for Senate. In 1968, he was the leading Democratic candidate for the Presidential Campaign.

On June 4, 1968, Bobby Kennedy defeated Eugene McCarthy in the California primaries. A few minutes past midnight on June 5, 1968, Kennedy was addressing his supporters from the Ambassador Hotel's main ballroom in Los Angeles, California. Sirhan Bishara Sirhan, a young Palestinian national who had Jordanian citizenship, opened fire on the crowd and fatally wounded Bobby Kennedy, who died from his injuries the very next day.

Sirhan Sirhan was convicted of the killing of Bobby Kennedy. He officially became the second lone shooter with no ulterior motive to kill a Kennedy brother.

But unofficially, who benefitted from Bobby Kennedy's death?

Just like his brother John, Bobby was straying from the Illuminati's main ideology, the idea of a New World Order. The same Illuminati who, just like John, had put him in power for a reason and now Bobby was going against everything that they backed.

If elected President of the United States, Bobby Kennedy planned on renewing his brother's policies in Southeast Asia, and of course he planned on continuing his ruthless crackdown on organized crime. These were two of the main reasons why JFK was assassinated. It would only make sense that Bobby was eliminated for the same reasons, by the same people, wouldn't it?

Therefore, the CIA took matters into their own hands and with the help of Mossad (the Israeli national intelligence agency), groomed the perfect scapegoat for the task. They found a young, impressionable man who was instilled a deep hatred of Kennedy. Bobby Kennedy's campaign headquarters had been infiltrated by a sympathizer of the Shah of Iran, and therefore Mossad and the CIA knew exactly where and when to strike.

Sirhan Sirhan was told that Bobby Kennedy was about to send 50 bombers over Israel to take care of the Middle East problems, and the young Palestinian took it as a affront to his nation. He got his hands on (was given?) a shotgun and he killed Bobby Kennedy so he would not send bombers over Israel and Palestine. June 5th was significant because it was the anniversary of the victory of Israel over the Arabs.

At least, that is the story he has been feeding the authorities since that tragic night.

The Assassination of John F. Kennedy Jr.

John F. Kennedy Jr. affectionately known as "John John" was three days shy of his third birthday when his father was assassinated on November 22, 1963. Everyone remembers the iconic image of little John John saluting his father's casket on his third birthday, with his grieving mother Jacqueline Bouvier Kennedy and his older sister Caroline by his side.

After his father's death, JFK Jr. went on to live in New York City, with his mother and her new husband, Aristotle Onassis of the Illuminati Onassis bloodline and a Greek shipping tycoon. The Secret Service protection that had been granted him ended on his 16th birthday in 1976.

John F. Kennedy Jr. became a lawyer and despite publicly denouncing his interests in an immediate political career, JFK Jr. was indeed planning to make his political entrance. As a matter of fact, he was Editor in Chief and 50% owner of the magazine *George* which was supposed to praise politics as a lifestyle.

In the publication, JFK Jr., who was unafraid of scandal and not easily threatened, had in mind to uncover some secrets regarding his father's death. Rumor has it that he was on the verge of naming the names of the conspirators. While most involved in the 1963 assassination were dead by 1999, George Bush Sr., who had been a high ranking CIA operative in 1963, and of course the 41st President of the United States, knew that much was at stake. Indeed, photographic evidence placed him in Dallas on November 22, 1963.

In addition to the damage he could have done by spilling his secrets, and according to government whistleblower Sherman Skolnick, JFK Jr. planned to reveal a well-kept secret that on or about August 1, 1999, JFK JR. was to announce that he would be running for President as a traditional Democrat or in view of the distrust of both parties, to run as a independent on a third party ticket.

However, this plan would have been detrimental to George W. Bush, the Governor of Texas, the son of George Bush Sr. George W. Bush evidently wanted the Presidency, and was ready to stop at nothing to get what he wanted.

On July16, 1999, John F. Kennedy Jr. his wife Caroline Bessette Kennedy and his sister-in-law Lauren Bessette boarded a Pipe Saratoga plane, piloted by John John himself.

John Kennedy Jr. was an experienced pilot, who had over 300 flight hours under his belt. Flying to Martha's Vineyard, an airfield in which he was very familiar, with. The day was clear and sunny. The FAA (Federal Aviation Administration) has reported since that his on-board instruments worked well since the control tower was in constant communication with him and received appropriate readings throughout his approach of the runway.

A careful pilot, despite ill-intended rumors that his wife was scared to fly with him, John John knew what he was doing. With his plane showing no evident signs of stalling or malfunction, as erroneously reported in certain media, John F. Kennedy Jr. was en route to his cousin Rory's wedding, in good spirits and ready to land smoothly.

Yet his plane missed the runway and crashed into the ocean, killing all three occupants on impact.

How could this happen?

A witness said the weather was conducive of a good landing, with only a little haze on the horizon, thus refuting the widely circulated theory that JFK Jr. lost the horizon due to the haze. Also, it was said that the supposedly reckless pilot lost control of his plane. How could that be and he had over 300 flight hours and was well qualified to be a commercial pilot? The plane was practically new, making the theory of an equipment malfunction quasi-impossible.

The theory of the accidental crash has so many flaws in it. It just does not make sense.

What makes sense, however, is the fact that just two days before the "accident", an agent of Mossad the Israeli intelligence office was seen at the Essex County airport where JFK Jr. kept his plane.

A long list of witnesses were interviewed in conjunction with the crash. A dozen people reported hearing an explosion right before the crash and a dozen more said they actually saw the plane explode in mid-air. The plane blew up while still in the air, not on impact! Additionally, several credible sources were quoted as saying that the debris and the bodies were consistent with a mid-air explosion, not disintegration on impact with water.

Between the eye witnesses and the evidence pointing at John F. Kennedy Jr.'s intentions to follow in his father's footsteps, it is easily to surmise that he, too like his father and uncle was assassinated because his potential to disrupt the plans of the Illuminati and their New World Order.

Chapter 7: The Assassination of Malcolm X

Malcolm X was born Malcolm Little in Omaha, Nebraska on May 19, 1925 and was the son of Louise and Earl Little who was a Baptist minister and a follower of Black nationalist leader Marcus Garvey's Universal Negro Improvement Association (UNIA) which stated goal was to return black people to their ancestral homeland of Africa. Their slogans included "Africa for the Africans" and "Ethiopians Unite". Through his father's activities and involvement with Garvey's organization young Malcolm got his first exposure to the concept of "black pride" and "black determination". Earl Little was eventually murdered and his family believed that he was murdered by the White supremacist group the Black Legions because of his involvement with Marcus Garvey's organization.

Malcolm's mother eventually had a nervous breakdown and was committed to a mental institution. Malcolm had the dream of being a lawyer but dropped out of junior high school when a teacher told him that was "no realistic goal for a nigger". Eventually Malcolm was sent to Boston at the age of 15 to live with his half sister Ella after living in a series of foster homes. Ella was a strong woman, but she couldn't control Malcolm and he gravitated towards the street life of Boston engaging in criminal activity. After committing a series of crimes, he was eventually arrested for burglary, convicted and was sent to prison. He received an 8-10 year sentence.

While serving his sentence Malcolm was introduced to the teachings of the Honorable Elijah Muhammad leader of the Nation of Islam by his brother Reginald. Attracted to the Nation of Islam's message that "the Whiteman was the Devil", Malcolm converted to Islam while in prison and became a Black Muslim and a member of the Nation of Islam. Also during this time in prison he began corresponding with Elijah Muhammad via letter. He changed his name from Malcolm Little to Malcolm X. The "X" represented the unknown name of his African ancestors and the culture that was lost during slavery. In his autobiography, he stated "For me, my 'X' replaced the white slave master name of 'Little' which some blue-eyed devil named Little had imposed upon my paternal forebears."

Malcolm X was paroled from prison in 1952 and eventually met Elijah Muhammad who shortly thereafter in 1953 made him assistant minister of Nation of Islam's Temple No. 1 in Detroit and Malcolm relentlessly recruited new members. Later in the same year Malcolm established Temple No. 11 in Boston and a year later he established Temple No. 12 in Philadelphia. Malcolm was chosen by Elijah Muhammad to lead Temple No. 7 in Harlem, New York where Malcolm expanded its membership as black people joined in droves. Malcolm became more and more visible to the public because of his great oratory skills. He was a charismatic and fiery speaker.

However, as a result of its increasing membership and its philosophies, the Nation of Islam attracted the attention of the FBI's Director J. Edgar Hoover and he began devising counterintelligence schemes to thwart the Nation of Islam's growth. I also must note that while in prison Malcolm wrote President Harry Truman a letter expressing opposition to the Korean War which prompted the FBI to open up a file on him. After he was appointed assistant minister in Detroit, Malcolm made the FBI's DETCOM (Detention of Communists) and COMSAB (Communist Sabotage) lists. The FBI then began bugging all of the Nation of Islam's mosques putting its members, Elijah Muhammad and Malcolm X under surveillance.

Needless to say the United States government and its intelligence agencies like the FBI and the CIA saw the rise and the growing popularity of Elijah Muhammad, Malcolm X and the Nation of Islam as a threat and they worked hard day and night to discredit and infiltrate the organization with the intentions of dismantling and destroying it. You didn't have to look very far to see what the Nation of Islam believed and wanted for Black people in America as its doctrine was published in their newspaper called Muhammad Speaks in which Malcolm contributions helped make it the largest circulating Black newspaper of that day. The following represents one of the tenets of their "What the Muslims Want" doctrine which must have surely alarmed the intelligence agencies of the United States government as well as the white power structure:

"We want our people in America whose parents or grandparents were descendants from slaves, to be allowed to establish a separate state or territory of their own…either on this continent or elsewhere. We believe that our former slave masters are obliged to provide such land and that the area must be fertile and minerally rich. We believe that our former slave masters are obligated to maintain and supply our needs in this separate territory for the next 20 to 25 years…until we are able to produce our own needs. Since we cannot get along with them in peace and equality, after giving them 400 years of our sweat and blood, and receiving in return some of the worst treatment human beings have ever experienced, we believe our contributions to this land and the suffering forced upon us by White America, justifies our demand for complete separation in a state or territory of our own."

As a result of his charisma, great oratory skills and him standing on the principles and teachings of Elijah Muhammad, Malcolm grew in popularity and became internationally acclaimed. He became one of the most sought after speakers at College campuses in the United States and he received a lot of press. However, as his popularity grew so did the jealousy within the Nation of Islam. Although Malcolm always said during interviews and debates that he represented Elijah Muhammad some people within the Nation of Islam felt that he was getting too much credit and acclaim which they felt should have been bestowed on Elijah Muhammad.

At this point in time the FBI and other intelligence agencies were successful in infiltrating the Nation of Islam. They had black agents who worked for them join the Nation of Islam and become members. Some of them were even able to get into the inner circle. Malcolm was even aware of this and he stated that some of these black agents came to him out of guilt and informed him that they were sent to infiltrate and disrupt the Nation of Islam's activities. However, Malcolm said with some of these agents he was able to turn them around and even had them counter spy on the intelligence organizations that they came from.

Nonetheless, the intelligence community of the United States government saw an opening as a result of this jealously and they worked hard to exacerbate it. The United States government through documents have also admitted to working on creating a division between Malcolm X and Elijah Muhammad. .They just needed the perfect moment and situation.

Malcolm X's Split with the Nation of Islam

The perfect moment for the government came when President John F. Kennedy was assassinated. Elijah Muhammad sent a message of condolence to the Kennedy family and instructed all of his ministers not to say anything about the assassination because the country was sensitive and in deep mourning. However, Malcolm X was asked by a reporter to give a comment on the Kennedy assassination and he said that it was a case of "chickens coming home to roost". He added that "chickens coming home to roost never did make me sad; they've always made me glad." These comments once they were reported infuriated the public. As a result of his comments about Kennedy's assassination Elijah Muhammad suspended Malcolm X from the Nation of Islam for 90 days and he was prohibited from speaking to the public.

Also during this time Malcolm X discovered through Wallace D. Muhammad Elijah Muhammad's son that Elijah Muhammad was engaged in extramarital affairs with several of his secretaries which would constitute a serious violation of the Nation of Islam's teachings.

On March 8, 1964 Malcolm X announced his split from the Nation of Islam and he formed the Muslim Mosque Inc. Shortly thereafter he also formed The Organization of Afro-American Unity (OAAU) which was modeled after the Organization of African Unity in Africa. In a memo dated July 2, 1964 the FBI's J. Edgar Hoover deemed the newly formed Organization of Afro-American Unity a threat to the national security of the United States.

Malcolm began to speak out publicly about this situation involving Elijah Muhammad which drew the ire of the members of the Nation of Islam who loved Elijah Muhammad. In an interview with Mike Wallace he asked Malcolm X the following question: "Are you not perhaps afraid of what might happen to you as a result of making these revelations?" Malcolm responded: "Oh, yes. I probably am a dead man already".

He further went on to say "if I myself by having confidence in the leader of the Muslim movement and someone came to me and I had no knowledge what so ever to what had taken place and they told me what I'm saying I'd would kill them, myself. The only thing that would prevent me from killing someone who made a statement like this they would have to be able to let me know that it is true. Now if anyone would have come to me other than Mr. Muhammad's son I never would have believed it, even enough to look into it. But I had been around him so closely I had seen indications of the reality of it but my religious sincerity made me block it out of my mind".

The FBI'S COINTELPRO

Meanwhile the FBI's counterintelligence program known as COINTELPRO went to work to fan the flames of enmity that developed between the devoted members of the Nation of Islam and Malcolm X. To understand how COINTELPRO actually fanned the flames of this situation you would have to first know what COINTELPRO is and why it existed in the first place. COINTELPRO created by J. Edgar Hoover was a series of covert, and at times illegal, projects conducted by the FBI aimed at surveying, infiltrating, discrediting, and disrupting domestic political organizations.

It targeted and went after groups and organizations that it deemed subversive and a threat to the national security of the United States. It first started targeting people and organizations who were considered to be Communist, but quickly turned its attention to the Civil Rights/ Black power movement and the FBI began a malicious campaign against the leaders of that movement which included Malcolm X, Elijah Muhammad, Martin Luther King Jr. as well as many others.

Some of the dirty tactics that COINTELPRO used for example was the drafting of fake letters that were critical of the Nation of Islam and Elijah Muhammad that appeared to be written by Malcolm but they were not. They would then send these letters to some of Malcolm's enemies inside the ranks of the National leadership of the Nation of Islam with the intentions of creating further discord and dissension. The FBI even planted false stories and information in the newspapers to create the same effect.

The Climate of Death

Many people inside the Nation of Islam were angered with Malcolm's split with the Nation and Elijah Muhammad and this created a climate of death that surrounded Malcolm. Minister Louis X of Boston known today as the Honorable Minister Louis Farrakhan and present leader of the Nation of Islam even admitted that although he did not kill Malcolm, he was one of the people that was responsible for creating the climate of death that surrounded Malcolm .X. In fact, the following quote comes from an article written by him on Dec 10, 1964 in an edition of the Muhammad Speaks newspaper.

"Only those who wish to be led to hell or to their doom will follow Malcolm. The die is set, and Malcolm shall not escape, especially after such evil foolish talk about his benefactor, Elijah Muhammad. Such a man as Malcolm is worthy of death, and would have met with death had it not been for Muhammad's confidence in Allah for victory over the enemies".

To give you a complete backdrop of the events that took place during this time period I must also note that Elijah Muhammad warned Nation of Islam members not to lay a hand on Malcolm.

Also during this time period, Malcolm X's house was firebombed and he said in a speech that "the Muslims claimed that I bombed my own house". However, as further events unfurled, Malcolm believed that US intelligence agencies were responsible for certain things because he said that he trained the Muslims and he knew what they could do and what they were capable of. He stated that the Muslims of the Nation of Islam didn't have the resources to finance a worldwide spy network.

For instance, he was poisoned while traveling abroad in Cairo, Egypt. He also stated that the CIA made their presence known to him and tried to intimidate him as he traveled throughout Africa to gain support from African leaders for his planned United Nations proposal to declare that the United States was guilty of violating Black people's human rights in America. Malcolm X was also barred from entering France and he was kept from leaving the airport and forced to fly directly back to Britain by French officials. France according to many historians knew of the plot by US intelligence agencies to assassinate Malcolm and they did not want it to occur on their soil and be blamed for it.

Malcolm X Assassinated

On February 21, 1965 Malcolm X was scheduled to speak at a regular meeting of the Organization of Afro American Unity (OAAU) at the Audubon Ballroom in Harlem. When he arrived at the Audubon he went backstage and immediately remarked to an aid "I really shouldn't be here today" because he felt that something evil was about to go down. All the speakers who were scheduled to speak that day mysteriously canceled at the last minute. The crowd grew restless waiting for the activities to get started. After a brief introduction given by Benjamin X, Malcolm greeted the crowd in the Arabic words of peace "As-Salaam Alaikum and the audience responded back in kind "Wa-Alaikum Salaam".

As Malcolm continued to speak a bodyguard by the name of Gene Roberts who was stationed near him as he spoke made a request to be relieved of his post and he was replaced by another bodyguard. Gene Roberts then took another position at the front entrance. Mysteriously uniform police officers who were stationed at all of Malcolm's events were nowhere to be found as they had left the area.

A commotion broke out in the middle section of the audience and two men began scuffling. One of them shouted "nigger get your hand out of my pocket" Malcolm tried to stop them by saying "hold it" and he extended his hands towards the two men. As he did that a Black man sitting in the front row pulled a gun and shot Malcolm X in the chest. Then another Black man rose out of the third row with a shot gun in hand fired at Malcolm and hit him in the chest and Malcolm slumped to the floor. As he fell to the floor a third gunman shot him in his leg and hand. A fourth gunman made his way back to the front entrance and began firing multiple shots at Malcolm X. Malcolm X hit the floor and was bleeding profusely from his gunshot wounds.

One of Malcolm X's bodyguards began firing shots at Malcolm's assailants striking one of them. Members of the audience began attacking the wounded man who later was identified as 22 year old Talmadge Hayer a member of the Nation of Islam. The remaining gunmen escaped by brandishing their weapons to the crowd. Gene Roberts who was stationed at the front entrance ran back to the stage and appeared to be giving Malcolm X mouth to mouth resuscitation. Betty Shabazz, Malcolm X's wife and a nurse pushed Gene Roberts out of the way and attempted to save her husband's life.

Some men ran over to the nearby Presbyterian hospital to seek assistance. They got no response from the staff and after waiting a few minutes they snatched a stretcher from the emergency room and went back to the Audubon and with the assistance of others who were in the audience lifted Malcolm X and placed him on the stretcher. But when they proceeded to carry him out they were intercepted by uniformed police officers who ordered them to step aside. The police officers took Malcolm X to the hospital where after 15 minutes he was pronounced dead at the age of 39.

Norman 3X Butler and Thomas 15X Johnson members of the Nation of Islam were later arrested for the murder of Malcolm X. Talmadge Hayer, Butler and Thomas stood trial and were convicted of the murder of Malcolm X. Hayer admitted in affidavits that both Butler and Thomas were both innocent, were not at the scene of the crime and did not participate in the assassination. He claimed that Leon David, Wilbur McKinley, William Bradley, and Benjamin Thomas from the Nation of Islam Temple no. 25 located in Newark, New Jersey had participated in the crime.

The Greater Conspiracy

Although members of the Nation of Islam did fire the guns that killed Malcolm X, there were hidden forces manipulating the events behind the scenes. Gene Roberts, Malcolm X's chief of security who relieved himself of his post standing next to Malcolm right before Malcolm was shot and gave Malcolm mouth to mouth resuscitation was an undercover NYPD police officer. Roberts was an agent with NYPD's Bureau of Special Services (BOSS), a super-secret political intelligence unit nicknamed the "Red Squad." Many people have asserted that while Roberts appeared to be giving mouth to mouth resuscitation to Malcolm he was really checking Malcolm's vital signs. Roberts as an undercover agent later on went to infiltrate and disrupt the Black Panther Party.

What about the FBI's involvement? It is already documented in declassified documents that J. Edgar Hoover and the FBI targeted the Nation of Islam, Elijah Muhammad, and Malcolm X through COINTELPRO. Author Louis Lomax in his book even stated that John Ali the then national secretary of the Nation of Islam was a former FBI agent and informant who had infiltrated the Nation of Islam's inner circle.

What about the CIA's involvement? Malcolm became an even bigger threat to the United States once he began to speak out boldly against colonialism in Africa. He also was considered to be an even greater threat when he garnered the support of eight African nations to take the case of Black America to the United Nations as a human rights case as opposed to a civil rights case. In fact, Malcolm X was the only American that was allowed to be heard at the Organization of African Unity meeting. Malcolm X was also close to forming an alliance with the Reverend Dr. Martin Luther King Jr. and that alliance would have been a formidable foe for the Unites States government and the White power structure in America and throughout the world.

Malcolm X became such a concern for the United States government that CIA director Richard Helms instructed his agents to do everything they could to "monitor" his activities. Minister Louis Farrakhan in a speech he gave summed up the greater conspiracy. He stated the following:

"This conspiracy started with the government of the United States because of its hatred of the movement that Malcolm X and the Honorable Elijah Muhammad had generated and the effect that these two men were having on Black America. J Edgar Hoover was determined that no black messiah would rise to unite our people in their quest for justice and true liberation. Untold sums of tax payer dollars were used by the FBI to hurt the legitimate movement of our people toward liberation. Our zeal, our love, and hatred, our ignorance were manipulated by powerful outside forces and the result is that members of the Nation of Islam were involved in the assassination of Malcolm X. And the Nation has taken the heat and carried the burden of the murder of Malcolm X. We can not deny whatever our part was, that is true but we must not let the real culprit get away hiding his hand and keep us fighting and killing one another".

In the same speech he went on to say:

"We want the files on Malcolm X to be opened so that the world may see the real truth of what went down. We want the truth to be made known so that we as a people can be made free of suspicion and of doubt and let the truth condemn whomever truth would condemn. But the people must go free and we in the Nation of Islam as well as those outside of the Nation of Islam need to know all of the truth as it relates to the assassination of brother Malcolm X".

Chapter 8: The Assassination of Dr. Martin Luther King Jr.

The 60's were a time period of consciousness that spawned a movement in which individuals and organizations sought change through protest and action. Some believed like Malcolm X did that if you couldn't accomplish change through the ballot, the only other way that change would come was by the bullet. There were others who took a more nonviolent approach and the way that they sought change was through peaceful civil disobedience. The Rev. Martin Luther King Jr. adopted the latter approach as a strategy in his quest for civil rights. He preferred the "turn the other cheek" approach which he modeled after Ghandi in an effort to turn his aggressors' violence against them.

However, despite using the tactic of passive resistance in an effort to seek change and free black people and other races from the yoke of oppression and social injustice, Martin Luther King Jr. was still seen as a threat to the status quo and the white power structure. But who exactly was Martin Luther King Jr. and why was he considered a powerful threat to the national security of the United States?

Martin Luther King Jr. was born Michael King (his father later changed his name to Martin) on January 15, 1929 in Atlanta, Georgia. His father, grandfather and his great grandfather were Christian Baptist ministers so to no one's surprise he followed in their footsteps. He attended the famed Morehouse College in Atlanta and received his first exposure to civil rights through his father and grandfather, who were both leaders of the Atlanta branch of the NA.ACP. They fought against racial discrimination in voting and teacher's salaries and this served as a model for the younger Martin.

During his time at Morehouse, King took his first steps toward political activism. In response to the increasing anti-black postwar violence King wrote a letter to the editor of the Atlanta Constitution newspaper decrying these heinous acts. He stated in his letter that black people were "entitled to the basic rights and opportunities of American citizens." At the end of his senior year at Morehouse, King became an ordained minister. After graduating at the top of his class at Morehouse, King attended Boston University's School of Theology where he pursued his doctoral studies in systematic theology.

Upon graduating and receiving his doctorate at Boston University, King decided to become pastor of Dexter Avenue Baptist Church in Montgomery, Alabama. During this time segregation was the law of the land in the United States and blacks and whites could not go to the same schools, drink at the same water fountain, use the same public toilets, eat at the same restaurants and black people were forced to ride at the back of the bus in the "colored" section while white people sat at the front. However, in regards to the latter a woman by the name of Rosa Parks one day refused an order from the bus driver to give up her seat to a white man in Montgomery, Alabama and as a result of her refusal she was arrested.

In response to this Montgomery black leaders Jo Ann Robinson, E. D. Nixon, and Ralph Abernathy formed the Montgomery Improvement Association (MIA) to protest the arrest of Rosa Parks and they chose Dr. Martin Luther King Jr. to head this new group and guide the Montgomery Bus Boycott. During the Montgomery Bus protest King used his religious Christian training and his leadership skills to mobilize the black churches in Montgomery and to appeal for white support. The Montgomery Bus Boycott turned into a massive 13 month protest and it resulted in the US Supreme Court ruling that segregation on public buses was unconstitutional.

Encouraged by the Montgomery Bus Boycott results, King expanded his nonviolent civil rights movement throughout the South and along with C. K. Steele, Fred Shuttlesworth and T J.

Jemison and others founded the Southern Christian Leadership Conference (SCLC) which he was made the president of. Although the Southern Christian Leadership Conference was birthed out of the Montgomery Bus Boycott it expanded its focus beyond busses to ending all forms of segregation.

SCLC also organized the nonviolent protests in Birmingham, Alabama which gained national attention after television news coverage showed the brutal police response to these nonviolent protests. Images flooded the television screens across America showing police dogs being sic on unarmed black men, women and children. Fire hoses with water being sprayed on the retreating protesters and police officers mercilessly beating to a pulp the nonviolent protesters. There were some black leaders who vehemently disagreed with King's nonviolent passive approach in the face of violence and his integrationist agenda. One of those leaders was Malcolm X who stated the following on the subject of nonviolence:

"It is criminal to teach a man not to defend himself, when he is the constant victim of brutal attacks".

"It doesn't mean that I advocate violence, but at the same time, I am not against using violence in self-defense. I don't call it violence when it's self-defense, I call it intelligence".

Nonetheless, Martin Luther King Jr. rocketed to national prominence and was recognized as a national civil rights leader. He also attracted the support of white liberals. However, just like Malcolm X he was targeted by J. Edgar Hoover and the FBI's COINTELPRO. He was under intense surveillance and they sent him threatening letters which included a letter and a cassette tape that allegedly contained audio of the married King with various women in different hotels rooms. The tone of the letter that was sent to King suggested that he commit suicide to save himself from the embarrassment. Here is an excerpt from that portion of the letter that suggests that he commit suicide:

"King, there is only one thing left for you to do. You know what it is. You have just 34 days in which to do it (this exact number has been selected for a specific reason, it has definite practical significance). You are done. There is but one way out for you. You better take it before your filthy, abnormal fraudulent self is bared to the nation".

The FBI even tried to paint Martin Luther King as a communist which they found no evidence of. Hoover and the FBI fanatically pursued King looking for possible angles to destroy him and the civil rights movement. A month before the famous March on Washington, Hoover sent a request to the then Attorney General Robert Kennedy to tap King's and his associates telephone lines. Hoover also filed a request to bug their homes and offices as well. Not only did Robert Kennedy agree to Hoover's request, but he also gave the FBI permission to break into King's home and offices to install the bugs.

After the March on Washington in August of 1963 where he gave his famous "I have a dream" speech, The FBI in a memo adamantly called King " the most dangerous and effective Negro leader in the country". When Martin Luther King won the Nobel Peace prize in 1964, Hoover was livid and ramped up efforts against King.

COINTELPRO

A few years later in a FBI memo dated March 4, 1968 the FBI stated what the goals of COINTELPRO were in regards to King, the civil rights movement and black nationalists groups.

1. Prevent the coalition of black nationalists groups.
2. Prevent the rise of a black messiah "who could unify, and electrify, the militant black nationalists movement". In regards to this particular goal the memo stated "Malcolm X might have been such a "messiah;" he is the martyr of the movement today. Martin Luther King, Stokely Carmichael and Elijah Muhammad all aspire to this

position. Elijah Muhammad is less of a threat because of his age. King could be a very real contender for this position should he abandon his supposed "obedience" to "white, liberal doctrines" (nonviolence) and embrace black nationalism".

3. Prevent violence on the part of black nationalists groups.
4. Prevent militant black nationalists groups and leaders from gaining by discrediting them to three separate segments of the community. The goal of discrediting black nationalists must be handled tactically in three ways. You must discredit those groups and individuals to, first, the responsible Negro community. Second, they must be discredited to the white community, both the responsible community and to "liberals" who have vestiges of sympathy for militant black nationalists simply because they are Negroes.
5. A final goal should be to prevent the long-range GROWTH of militant black organizations, especially among youth.

As time progressed, Martin Luther King Jr. began to move in another direction. He began questioning whether passive resistance was the right approach. He began to speak out against the war raging in Vietnam. In a speech entitled "A Time to Break Silence" delivered at Riverside Church in New York City on April 4, 1967 King criticized the hypocrisy of the war. He stated the following:

"We were taking the black young men who had been crippled by our society and sending them eight thousand miles away to guarantee liberties in Southeast Asia which they had not found in southwest Georgia and East Harlem. And so we have been repeatedly faced with the cruel irony of watching Negro and white boys on TV screens as they kill and die together for a nation that has been unable to seat them together in the same schools. And so we watch them in brutal solidarity burning the huts of a poor village, but we realize that they would hardly live on the same block in Chicago. I could not be silent in the face of such cruel manipulation of the poor."

In the same speech which definitely alarmed the corporations and the profiteers of the Vietnam War (i.e. the Illuminati) he defined his "true revolution of values". Here is a partial excerpt of what he said:

"A true revolution of values will soon look uneasily on the glaring contrast of poverty and wealth. With righteous indignation, it will look across the seas and see individual capitalists of the West investing huge sums of money in Asia, Africa, and South America, only to take the profits out with no concern for the social betterment of the countries, and say, "This is not just." It will look at our alliance with the landed gentry of South America and say, "This is not just." The Western arrogance of feeling that it has everything to teach others and nothing to learn from them is not just.

A true revolution of values will lay hand on the world order and say of war, "This way of settling differences is not just." This business of burning human beings with napalm, of filling our nation's homes with orphans and widows, of injecting poisonous drugs of hate into the veins of peoples normally humane, of sending men home from dark and bloody battlefields physically handicapped and psychologically deranged, cannot be reconciled with wisdom, justice, and love. A nation that continues year after year to spend more money on military defense than on programs of social uplift is approaching spiritual death".

Obviously War is big business. There are those like the Rothschilds and others who make huge sums of money from financing both sides of a conflict by charging an exorbitant amount of interest. Then there is the military industrial complex who also make huge sums of money from the manufacturing and selling of weapons of mass destruction. So it was in their best interests that the war in Vietnam was prolonged and by Martin Luther King Jr. who now was a highly visible and respected worldwide leader speaking out against it threatened the continuance of it. Many people around King believed that by making this speech and speaking out against the war in Vietnam King basically signed his own death warrant. I believe that he knew this also.

In addition to speaking out against the war in Vietnam, King along with the Southern Christian Leadership Conference organized the "Poor People's Campaign" to address the issues of economic injustice and the housing of the poor of all races. He planned another March on Washington just like the one that he had help organized in 1963, but this new March he planned was for the poor. King was seeking a 30 billion dollar a year program that included a plan for full employment and a guaranteed income for all. He also wanted to create an Economic Bill of Rights. His aggressive stance on these matters would lead to the inevitable.

On March 29, 1968 Martin Luther King Jr. traveled to Memphis, Tennessee to support black sanitation workers who went on strike to protest their poverty wages and horrible working conditions. On April 3, King delivered his "I've been to the mountain speech" at a rally and in the close of this particular speech he made reference to a previous bomb threat that delayed his flight to Memphis. King in reference to the bomb threat said the following:

"And then I got to Memphis. And some began to say the threats, or talk about the threats that were out. What would happen to me from some of our sick white brothers?

Well, I don't know what will happen now. We've got some difficult days ahead. But it doesn't matter with me now. Because I've been to the mountaintop. And I don't mind. Like anybody, I would like to live a long life. Longevity has its place. But I'm not concerned about that now. I just want to do God's will. And He's allowed me to go up to the mountain. And I've looked over. And I've seen the promised land. I may not get there with you. But I want you to know tonight, that we, as a people, will get to the promised land. So I'm happy, tonight. I'm not worried about anything. I'm not fearing any man. Mine eyes have seen the glory of the coming of the Lord".

Assassinated

This was a statement from a proud and spiritual man who knew that the end was near. On April 4, King was booked in room 306 at the Lorrain Motel. At 6:01 pm a sniper's shot rang out and Martin Luther King was hit while standing on the second floor balcony. The bullet went straight through his right cheek and traveled all the way down to his spine. He was taken to St Joseph's Hospital where after undergoing emergency chest surgery was pronounced dead at 7:05 pm.

There were many race riots that occurred throughout US cities as a result of Martin Luther King's assassination. The supposed shooter according to the "official" story was James Earl Ray, a petty criminal who was captured two months later after the assassination at London Heathrow airport while trying to leave the United Kingdom on a false Canadian passport in the name of Ramon George Sneyd. James Earl Ray was quickly extradited to Tennessee and charged with Martin Luther King's murder.

The Conspiracy

William F. Pepper (a King family attorney) stated in his book "An Act of State: The Execution of Martin Luther King that James Earl Ray was represented by an attorney who was connected to the actual killers. This lawyer told James Earl Ray that he would be famous and get off with a light sentence if he pled guilty to murdering King. Ray pled guilty and was sentenced to 99 years in prison. James Earl Ray just like Lee Harvey Oswald was nothing more than a "patsy" who was setup to take the fall. However, Ray realized he was tricked and just three days later after pleading guilty he tried to withdraw his guilty plea and his request was denied.

It gets even deeper. James Earl Ray later claimed that a man he met in Montreal, Canada with the alias of Raoul was involved in the assassination of King and that the assassination in itself was the result of a conspiracy. Could this have been the same Raoul who was one of "The Tramps" that I mentioned earlier in the John F. Kennedy assassination? Hmmm....

And what about King's security detail? Where were they? Ed Reddit a black police detective of the Memphis Police Department who was assigned to the security detail of King was removed from that detail two hours before King was assassinated and sent home and the reason that was given to him was that a threat had been made against his life.

Another black Memphis Police Department detective Jerry Williams who was usually in charge of forming a security team of black police officers every time King came to Memphis testified in court in the 1999 civil trial of the King Family versus Jowers and Other Unknown Co-Conspirators that on the day of the assassination he wasn't assigned that task. We will get to who Jowers was and what role he played shortly.

In addition to all of this, the police escort that accompanied King's security detail was mysteriously pulled back. So in essence Martin Luther King was left vulnerable, and unprotected, the perfect recipe for assassination. Also people who could have been potential witnesses to the assassination were out the way and that included two firemen Floyd Newsum and Norvell Wallace who were working at fire station #2 located across the street from the Lorrain motel. Both Newsum and Wallace were transferred from fire station #2 to different fire stations. In the aforementioned civil trial Newsum testified that he wasn't actually needed at the fire stationed he was transferred to and as a result of his transfer meant that no one would be at fire station #2 unless someone was sent there. He also stated that he inquired as to why he was being transferred and the explanation that he was given was that it was ordered by the Memphis Police Department.

How Martin Luther King was setup

Loyd Jowers was the owner of Jim Grill's restaurant located near the Lorraine Motel. His business was used as a staging area for planning King's assassination. He ran a café on the ground floor which the corporate controlled Illuminati media claimed was where a single shot was fired by a sniper supposedly James Earl Ray that resulted in Dr. Martin Luther King's death. To give you an idea of Jowers background he was a police officer for the Memphis Police Department in the 1940's.

In a 1993 television interview on ABC show Prime Time Live Jowers said that he received $100,000 from Frank Liberto who was a Memphis produce merchant and had mafia connections to arrange Dr. Martin Luther King's murder. He also stated in the same interview that he was given the money to hire the assassin and James Earl Ray was not the shooter and did not murder Dr. King, however he was made the scapegoat.

In 1998, the King family filed a wrongful death suit against Jowers and other known conspirators for the assassination and murder of Dr. Martin Luther King. At trial, William F. Pepper the King family attorney played an incriminating audio of a conversation between Dexter King (Martin Luther King's son), UN Ambassador Andrew Young and Jowers where Jowers stated that " he wanted to get right with God before he died, wanted to confess it and be free of it".

On the tape he also stated that a meeting took place at Jim's Café to plan the assassination. He also named the planners at that meeting which included Memphis Police Department officer

Merrell McCollough (who later worked for the CIA), Memphis Police Department Lieutenant Earl Clark, another Memphis Department police officer and two men who Jowers believed were Federal Agents. On the same tape Andrew Young was heard identifying McCollough as the man kneeling besides Dr. King's body on the balcony in that famous photograph of the event.

Jowers also made this stunning admission on the tape that right after the shot was fired he received a smoking rifle at the rear door of Jim's Grill from Earl Clark. He then proceeded to break the rifle down in two pieces and wrapped it in a table cloth. He then said that Raoul picked the rifle up the next day. Although Jowers did not see who fired the shot he believe it was Earl Clark because Clark was known as Memphis Police Department's best marksman.

Another interesting note is that while in Memphis Dr. Martin Luther King was under open Federal surveillance by the by the 111th Military Intelligence Group based at Fort McPherson in Atlanta, Georgia. Also during his last visit to Memphis before he was assassinated, Dr. King was under covert surveillance which meant that the hotel room he was in at the Rivermont hotel was bugged and wired. In his closing arguments of the Jowers civil trial the plaintiff's attorney William Pepper implied that this covert surveillance meant that there were at least two Federal Agencies involved because this type of surveillance was usually done by the by the Army Security Agency.

The Government Found Guilty In The Conspiracy

When the civil trial concluded a jury found local, state, and federal government agencies and Jowers guilty of conspiring to assassinate Dr. Martin Luther King. But you didn't hear about this right? The jury's verdict should have been blasted all over the Illuminati controlled corporate media, but it wasn't.

At a press conference after the verdict Dr. King's widow Coretta Scott King said the following:

"There is abundant evidence of a major high level conspiracy in the assassination of my husband, Martin Luther King, Jr. The conspiracy of the Mafia, local, state and federal government agencies were deeply involved in the assassination of my husband. The jury also affirmed overwhelming evidence that identified someone else, not James Earl Ray, as the shooter, and that Mr. Ray was set up to take the blame.

Chapter 9: The Assassination of Pope John Paul I

Pope John Paul I was the head of the Roman Catholic Church from his election to papacy by the conclave of Cardinals on August 26, 1978 to his untimely death on September 28, 1978.

His reign as Pope was one of the shortest in the history of the Church, resulting in the first Year of Three Popes since 1605.

John Paul I was the first pope to be born in the 20th century and the last pope to die in it. In fact, he is the only pope to have lived his entire life in the 20th century. He was also the last Italian-born Pope to have been elected after a long tradition of Italian pontiffs that had started with Clement VII in 1523.

At first reluctant to accept the title of Pope if elected by the conclave upon the death of his predecessor Paul VI, Albino Luciani realized that it was his duty when after the ninth vote, the conclave decided upon his election.

A Pope known for his gentle manners and for being close to the people, Pope John Paul I was adored by all the Catholics around the world. At least, almost all the Catholics around the world.

Nicknamed Il Papa del Sorriso (The Smiling Pope) and Il Sorriso di Dio (The smile of God), Albino Luciani wanted to humanize the papacy and make his office more approachable. With modern, forward ideas such as the tolerance toward birth control, Pope John Paul I was definitely a revolutionary pontiff.

Officially, John Paul I was found dead, sitting upright in his bed, on the morning of September 28, 1978. It was the 33rd day of his papacy. It was reported by the Vatican that Pope John Paul I, a 65 year old healthy man, had died of natural causes, more precisely a heart attack.

Who found the Pope dead? It was Sister Vicenza, an Italian nun who worked in the papal apartments. She initially said she found the Pope dead in his bathroom around 4:45 AM on the morning of September 28, 1978. She later recalled that she found him in his bed, sitting upright. What, or rather who made her change her mind?

Enter Cardinal Villot. Cardinal Villot was a French bishop who was an emissary of the Illuminati. In July 1971 he had been appointed president of the newly-formed Pontifical Council Cor Unum. It was a position he held until 1978 when he resigned from it during the reign of Pope John Paul I. He then became the Vatican's Secretary of State.

What was the true timeline of events preceding his death?

The night before the Pope was found dead, Cardinal Villot had a meeting with Pope John Paul I. They parted way late in the evening.

The next morning, as was customary, Sister Vicenza walked into the Pope's chambers to tend to her morning housekeeping duties at 4:45 AM. As she did not find the Pope at his desk as normal, she ventured further in the apartment and discovered the Pope laying on the bathroom floor, dead. He was still wearing his papal robe from the night before.

In a panic, she called upon the Secretary of State, none other than Cardinal Villot, to obtain his assistance.

Cardinal Villot's first call was not to the Vatican's doctor. It was not to the Vatican's gendarmerie corps. It was not to the Swiss Guard. Indeed, Cardinal Villot thought it urgent that his first call upon hearing the devastating news should be to the embalmers. The embalmers? As a matter of fact, he went so far as to send a car to pick them up, and in what seems like defying all logic, they were in the papal apartments by 5 AM.

What happened during the subsequent hour, no one knows but the embalmers and Cardinal Villot. No one was allowed in the apartments, until at 6 AM, the Cardinal called Dr. Buzzonati. This was an odd move, as the head of the Vatican's medical team was not Dr. Buzzonati, but Professor Fontana. Professor Fontana was not informed of the Pope's ill-fate until much later.

Cardinal Villot did not inform the other Cardinals of the tragic situation until around 6:30 AM. That is almost two hours after the Pope was originally found dead, and one and a half hour after the embalmers had been fetched!

In a curious turn of events, Cardinal Villot proceeded to extend the order to scrub the papal apartments. By 6 PM on September 28, 1978, the 19 rooms of the apartments had been cleaned, emptied and readied for the next pope. Not only was this move unusual, it was also illegal considering that Pope John Paul I's cause of death had not yet officially determined by the authorities.

In addition, the embalmers had been ordered not to drain one drop of blood or any organs out of the Pope's body. Why? Could forensic evidence uncover the use of poison, by chance?

Unless there was something to hide, why rush and eliminate important evidence that could have helped determine what happened?

Of course, it is highly suspicious that the last man to have been seen with the Pope alive ordered all evidence to be destroyed.

But Cardinal Villot, well aware that people were talking, decided to come forth with a phony explanation for the Pope's death and the avoidance of any criminal investigation. He stated in the French regional newspaper Ouest-France that the Pope had been taking blood pressure pills. With his busy schedule, the Cardinal surmised that the Pope forgot he had already taken his medication (Effortil) and took a double dose, thus causing an overdose and a heart attack. He said that he wanted to avoid scandal and people gossiping that the Pope may have committed suicide.

How noble of him…

However, according to relatives of the late Pope, he was in excellent health and was not in need of blood pressure medication.

Interestingly, in its October 9, 1978 issue, Time Magazine published an article about the Pope's death, and declared, "In an earlier age so untimely a death might have stirred deep suspicions: *"If this were the time of the Borgias," said a young teacher in Rome, "there'd be talk that John Paul was poisoned."*

Why would the illuminati want the Pope dead?

Simply put, Pope John Paul I stood in the way of everything the Illuminati wanted.

The Pope was highly vocal in his opposition to the Vatican Bank in its current state and wanted it cleaned up. As a matter a fact, Pope John Paul I may have based his dislike of the Vatican's bankers and financiers on insider information he was privy to. By1982, the Vatican Bank was riddled with scandals and corruption, with its ties to the Illuminati, the Freemasonry, the Mafia and the CIA. It was thought that the ultimate purpose of the Vatican Bank was to finance wars and genocides throughout the Third World, to indebt countries to the Illuminati and their cohorts. Several French and Italian reports at the time showed that over 150 high ranking Bishops and Cardinals were Freemasons and members of other dark secret societies.

The newly elected Pope was a sworn enemy of the Illuminati as he was passionately against the New World Order.

Pope John Paul I, the Smiling Pope, God's Smile, was targeted on his 33rd day of papacy, 33 being of course a symbolic number for the Freemasons, as the 33rd degree of Freemasonry is the highest degree one can attain.

It will come to no surprise that Cardinal Villot was also a Jesuit, a Freemason and a member of the Illuminati.

Chapter 10: The Assassination of Jaime Roldós

Jaime Roldós Aguilera was born in the city of Guayaquil, Ecuador and he attended the University of Guayaquil where he studied jurisprudence and social science. He excelled in his studies and won many awards and scholarships. He got his real introduction into politics in 1962 when he married Marta Bucarám the niece of Assad Bucarám , the leader of the Concentración de Fuerzas Populares (Concentration of Popular Forces) a populist party that leaned strictly towards the left. In 1968, Roldós was endorsed by the Concentration of Popular Forces and he was elected to the Ecuadorean legislature. However, this legislature was suspended by President José María Velasco Ibarra in 1970.

Nonetheless, in 1976, a period in which Ecuador was ruled by a military junta, Roldós began making more political strides as he was appointed to one of the three committees that was in charge of making changes to Ecuador's constitution as well as its election laws. As a result of these changes Ecuador adopted a new constitution in 1978. However, one of the clauses that was inserted in the new constitution by the military junta disqualified Assad Bucarám from the presidency in which he was heavily favored to win. So Roldós was endorsed by the Concentration of Popular Forces and ran instead on a populist platform.

The Hydrocarbons Policy

Jaime Roldós believed in helping the poor of Ecuador and he was both a nationalist and a populist and all about the Ecuadorean people and he deeply opposed the oil companies and multinational corporations that were rooted in Ecuador raping it for its natural resources and getting richer and richer while the poor received nothing and remained impoverished. One of the platforms that Roldós ran on in his run for President was the hydrocarbons policy which was based on the belief that Ecuador's greatest potential resource was petroleum and that the masses of Ecuadorean people should be largely the ones who benefitted from this valuable resource. He wanted the hydrocarbons policy to be the impetus for social reform but he was careful not to alienate the rich families of Ecuador who would have definitely given him trouble in his run for President.

He campaigned hard with the slogans "Roldós in office, Bucarám in power" and "The Force of Change" and he received 31% of the vote, but it wasn't the required 50% that he needed so he was forced into a run-off election. While the military junta delayed the run-off Roldós began building himself up amongst the people and eventually carved out his own identity escaping the shadow of Bucarám. Finally in 1979 the run-off election was held and Roldós received approximately 69% of the votes and defeated Sixto Durán Ballén, and became president on August 10, 1979.

From the very start of his Presidency Roldós encountered major problems. He fell into disfavor with Assad Bucarám and the Concentration of Popular Forces party within 20 days into his term, because of his refusal to carry out their agenda which he referred to as "the continuation of the status quo". Roldós then began his assault on the oil companies. In his inaugural address he stated the following:

"There are very positive indications of substantial petroleum reserves for which we will take firm and immediate steps at prospecting. In addition, we must take effective measures to defend the energy resources of the nation, that the State maintain the diversification of its exports and not lose its economic independence. The hydrocarbons policy will be managed with broad programmatic criteria. Our decisions will be inspired solely by national interests and in the unrestricted defense of our sovereign rights."

Texaco was the main beneficiary and key player in the oil game in Ecuador and Roldós wasted no time turning his sights on them, but Texaco rejected Roldós new initiatives and felt it would set a dangerous precedent if these bold new revolutionary initiatives came into existence because other countries would soon follow suit.

In 1981 Roldós presented his hydrocarbons law to Ecuador's congress and of course if this law was implemented it would have an adverse financial impact on the big oil companies like Texaco because Roldós demanded a greater share of the profits stating that he wanted to pull Ecuador and its people out of poverty. Of course this was met with great opposition by the big oil companies and they began a smear campaign against Roldós to discredit him and what he was proposing. They sent their powerful lobbyists to Washington and Quito, Ecuador with loads of bribe money to stop Roldós. They painted him as anti-American and anti-big business and said that he was another Fidel Castro.

However, Roldós wasn't intimidated despite the threats and he wouldn't back down. In fact, he got even bolder and spoke out against the conspiracy between politics, oil and religion. He accused the Summer Institute of Linguistics a missionary group of being a front organization who colluded with the oil companies. In the book Thy Will Be Done authors Gerald Colby and Charlotte Dennett point out that the Summer Institute of Linguistics founder William Cameron Townsend worked closely with the intelligence agencies most notably the CIA. In this book they also accused Townsend of working closely with Nelson Rockefeller of the Illuminati Rockefeller bloodline to hatch a systematic campaign to conquer and colonize the Amazon, displace the Amazonian people and steal their resources.

In John Perkins book Confessions of a Economic Hit Man he stated that whenever the Seismologist uncovered a possibility of oil under the surface in an area the Summer Institute of

Linguistics encouraged the native people of that area to move on to the missionary's reservations and "they would be given free food, shelter, medical treatment and a missionary style education" and in turn they had to deed their land over to the oil companies.

"Death by Airplane"

Roldós kicked the Summer Institute of Linguistics out of Ecuador and explicitly warned other foreign entities that if they had no intentions of helping Ecuador and the Ecuadorean people they would be expelled out of the country. As a result of what he stood for Roldas was marked for death.

On May 24, 1981 after giving a major speech and heading off to visit a community in southern Ecuador he died there in a fiery plane crash. The newspapers around the world screamed CIA assassination and of course this claim was ignored by the US press. John Perkins also stated in his book in regards to Roldós's death "I had no doubt that Roldós's death had not been an accident. It had all the markings of a CIA-orchestrated assassination. I understood that it had been executed so blatantly in order to send a message."

Chapter 11: The Assassination of Omar Torrijos

Omar Torrijos was born in the town of Santiago, Panama. Both of his parents were school teachers and he entered the ranks of the National Guard which was Panama's military force after going to a famous military school in El Salvador and receiving military training in both the United States and Venezuela. He quickly gained the respect of the poor and the dispossessed because he listened to their problems and showed a deep concern for them. In fact, he walked the streets of the slums and helped the unemployed find jobs as well as giving them financial assistance from his own pockets whenever he had the funds to do so. Through these great acts he became the champion of the poor.

Torrijos eventually reached the ranks of lieutenant colonel in the National Guard and in 1968 he and Major Boris Martinez were part of a coup that overthrew newly elected President Arnulfo Arias. After the successful coup Torrijos was named commander of the National Guard. Eventually a power struggle ensued between him and Martinez in which Torrijos was victorious. He exiled Martinez then promoted himself to Brigadier General.

Torrijos immediately began instituting social and economic reforms in Panama that highly benefitted the poor. There was land reform, labor reform, comprehensive health care and other significant initiatives instituted. But to truly understand Torrijos impact on Panama it is necessary to know the history of the Panama Canal. Before there was a Panama Canal ships had to sail 13,000 miles around the tip of South America to get to one ocean to another. So there was a need and desire to build a short cut.

In 1880, the French led by engineer Ferdinand de Lesseps tried first to build a Canal through the Central American isthmus to connect the Atlantic and Pacific Oceans. Panama was part of Colombia during the time the French undertook this venture. In 1889, after 22,000 deaths and pouring 250 million dollars into the building of the Canal the French were unsuccessful and gave up.

This inspired President Teddy Roosevelt. The United States Senate approved the Hay-Herran Treaty in 1903 approving the offering of a 10 million dollar payment to the Colombian government and annual payments of $250,000 for the aforementioned isthmus. The Colombian government refused to approve and ratify this treaty holding out for a $25 million dollar payment. As a result, President Roosevelt sent in the US warship Nashville which seized and killed a local militia commander and declared Panama an independent country. Also during this time, a revolt was taking place in Panama which undoubtedly was instigated by the United States.

Once Panama was declared an independent nation, a puppet government was immediately installed and the first Panama Canal treaty was signed. This treaty established a future American zone on both sides of the Canal. It also gave the United States the right to intervene militarily making Panama a US protectorate. The United States basically controlled Panama and its leaders who were put into place to strictly serve American interests which meant thwarting socialism, communism and any attempt to improve the lot of the poor Panamanians who basically worked as slaves for American corporations like United Fruit which was owned by Zapata Oil a company owned by the then US ambassador to the United Nations George H.W. Bush. The Panama Canal was eventually completed by the United States and it officially opened August 15, 1914.

Torrijos social and economic reforms weren't look upon favorably by the United States. Also looked upon with disfavor was Torrijos stance that Panama should have sovereignty over its own country, people and the Canal. He also did not like the fact the United States had the US Command Tropical Warfare Center and the School of the Americas located in the Canal Zone. These outfits were nothing more than training grounds for the children of Latin American dictators where they learned the science of warfare.

Forever Indebted to the Bankers

Torrijos understood clearly the game that the huge multinational companies like Bechtel played in developing nations like Panama. That game was to offer to build the infrastructure of a country via that country's taking out massive loans from illuminati outfits such as the World Bank and the Inter-American Development Bank. That money of course would be funneled back to the corporations like Bechtel and they derived huge profits while only a small few of the developing nation country's elite would get rich and benefit financially while the poor got nothing and were left hanging out to dry. The developing nation would then be saddled with debt that they could never repay. Their resources were usually taken over by the lending entities to be sucked dry by the corporations.

The goal with Panama was of course the same. However, according to John Perkins who wrote the book Confessions of an Economic Hitman and was the point man for consulting firm TS MAIN and was responsible for getting these type of contracts executed with Panama he and Torrijos had a deal in place. The deal was that Perkins would make an honest financial assessment of building such an infrastructure and in this assessment he would account for the poor of Panama. According to Perkins he did just that and the Torrijos government began awarding his company MAIN with contracts.

However, Torrijos plan to share the foreign aid with the poor of his country was seen as a threat to the global empire because that's not how the game is played. As I mentioned before the only people who usually benefitted from this" foreign aid" were the multinational corporations, the elite of the borrowing country and a few corrupted officials.

In the backdrop of all of this Torrijos was negotiating with President Jimmy Carter on new Panama Canal treaties. These negotiations produced two treaties which were signed by both the United States and Panama. The significance of these treaties was that they abrogated the Hay–Bunau-Varilla Treaty which was signed in 1903 by the United States and Panama which established the Panama Canal Zone and the construction of the Panama Canal. The treaties also guaranteed that Panama would gain control of the Canal after 1999. There was of course strong opposition to these new treaties.

Torrijos Marked for Death

When Ronald Reagan became President his administration wanted to renegotiate the treaties signed by Carter and Torrijos but Torrijos refused to do so. Torrijos list of enemies began to pile up. He was hated by powerful forces in the US military because of his stance on the School of the Americas and the US Command Tropical Warfare Center which were slated to close due to provisions he negotiated in the Torrijos-Carter Treaty.

He was hated according retired Colonel Roberto Diaz Herrera a cousin and former secretary of Torrijos because he tried to facilitate peaceful solutions to the existing conflicts that existed in Central America at that time. According to Diaz, Torrijos wanted to use his influence with both governments and guerillas to prevent radicalism leading to civil and political armed clashes that were taking place in the region. This was something that the United States vehemently opposed because they preferred a military defeat of the left.

Torrijos was also hated by the multinational corporations most notably by the Illuminati controlled Bechtel Group who were upset because Torrijos wanted the Japanese to replace the

Canal's structure which he deemed inefficient. This meant that Bechtel would have been excluded and would have missed out on making a ton of money.

How powerful is the Bechtel Group? Bechtel is the most influential engineering and Construction Company in the United States and the world. Its power interlocks with the United States government itself. Its senior officers like the late Casper Weinberger (President of Bechtel) and George Schulz (Vice President of Bechtel) ran Reagan's Presidential campaign and became members of his cabinet. Weinberger became Reagan's Secretary of Defense and Schulz became his Secretary of State. Donald Rumsfeld also a Bechtel man served as Secretary of Defense for President Gerald Ford and President George W. Bush.

Torrijos lack of compliance and his unwillingness to capitulate totally to the powerful Illuminati and their entities who are responsible for keeping the Global Empire intact and growing, meant that he was certainly marked for death. On July 31, 1981 Omar Torrijos died at age 52 when the airplane that he was traveling in a DeHavilland Twin Otter (DHC-6) was lost and crashed at Cerro Marta, in Coclesito, near Penonomé, Panama. He was killed just three months after the assassination of Jaime Roldós who had also succumbed to "Death by Airplane". The circumstances surrounding Torrijos death just like Roldós according to many reeked of a CIA assassination. Torrijos cousin Diaz stated in an interview with AFP that "Torrijos was a victim of a conspiracy planned by the CIA and a few Panamanians, with Noriega among them." In the same interview he also stated the following:

"The way they killed him was by placing a remote controlled explosive device onboard the plane."

"If you become an obstacle for the CIA, they simply eliminate you. Period!"

Diaz continued revealing more damaging information in regards to a CIA assassination plot in this particular interview. He alleged that prior to his death Torrijos was visited by a US intelligence operative who asked him to be cooperative with Washington and in exchange Panama wouldn't face any economic problems. He said that Torrijos refused and said the following to the operative "I'm not against your country, but I will not accept your impositions. I'm a man of my own decisions. You tell your people that"

So how does Manuel Noriega a lieutenant colonel under Torrijos figure in all of this? He immediately became the leader of Panama once Torrijos was assassinated. Noriega was also on the CIA payroll. When he was captured from Panama, tried and convicted in the United States for drug running it was revealed in court that he received almost 10 million dollars for his intelligence work with the CIA and according to Diaz, Torrijos never trusted Noriega. He said Torrijos was fully aware of Noriega ties to the drug cartels.

In fact, Diaz said that the CIA used Noriega in its sinister plan to deliver weapons financed by selling drugs to the opponents of the Sandinista government of Daniel Ortega. He went on to further say that Torrijos knew that the CIA and Noriega wanted him dead and that he often asked Noriega to fly with him. His reason for this? According to Diaz, Torrijos allegedly said to him "If he puts a bomb onboard the plane, he will have to remove it if he flies with me".

If there's any doubt to whether there was a CIA plot to assassinate Omar Torrijos here is the smoking gun. When Noriega was standing trial in the United States he had documents that showed that the United States government had plans to assassinate both him and Torrjos. His lawyer Frank Rubino who represented him at this trial stated to the court "General Noriega has in his possession documents showing attempts to assassinate General Noriega and Mr. Torrijos by agencies of the United States." The contents of these documents were never revealed in court because it was covered under the court's protective order, an obvious cover up.

The bottom line is that Omar Torrijos was assassinated because plain and simple the Illuminati and the Global Empire wanted him dead. He posed a serious threat to their power.

Chapter 12: The Murder of Princess Diana

On July 29, 1981, the world was captivated by the story of Diana Spencer, a kindergarten teacher, who was marrying Charles, Prince of Wales and heir to the throne of England, in St Paul's Cathedral in London. She was beautiful, young and had about her this genuine smile that made the masses fall in love with her.

Who was Lady Diana? She certainly was not the commoner that the press and the media would have had the people believe she was. Depicting her as a woman "like us" who landed the fairy tale life that was very lucrative. However, Diana Spencer was far from being "like us". Indeed, she was born The Honorable Lady Diana Spencer. Her father, Earl Spencer, was part of the Spencer Bloodline.

The Spencers are part an Elite bloodline that has spanned through the ages. They are cousins of the Churchhills who produced the fame British Prime Minister Wiinston Churchill. In fact, his full name was Sir Winston Leonard Spencer-Churchill. The Spencers are also related to Sir Robert Walpole, the Duke of Malborough and they married into the Cavendish family who are the Dukes of Devonshire. It gets even more interesting as Diana shares a common ancestry with Prince Charles. How? Through the 3rd Duke of Devonshire and also through King James I which connects her to the Merovingian of France.

Diana's brother, Charles, had for Godmother Queen Elizabeth II herself. So far from being a simple girl picked at random, Diana Spencer came from royal bloodlines and was accustomed to the high life and she use to spend her summers with the Royal Family while growing up.

It was not until 1980 that Charles showed a romantic interest in Diana. She had been invited to a ball at Buckingham Palace in honor of Charles' 30th birthday. Diana recalled later of that encounter that, "He leapt on me, practically." Following this awkward meeting, Charles and Diana were groomed to like each other by the Royal Family, who immediately saw in Diana the ideal Princess: she was cute, demure and malleable. During a stay at Balmoral, the Scottish estate of the Royals, Charles asked her hand in marriage and she accepted. The popular belief is that Diana at one point told Charles, "I love you so much," to which he replied cold heartedly, "Whatever love is."

Diana quickly realized that being engaged to the Prince of England was not all that glamorous. Photographers began following her around, recording her every move. Lady Di was not comfortable around her new found fame and she can be seen on many pictures sporting a shy smile. She was genuinely in love with Charles, but she certainly did not love the life associated with being the new Princess-to-be.

The wedding on July 29, 1981 was televised worldwide. This was truly THE wedding of the modern times. Young girls around the Globe fantasized about Diana's dream life while men admired Charles for his conquest. For Diana, however, her new life began with a cold realization. She said of her wedding day, "I felt I was a lamb to the slaughter. I knew it and I couldn't do anything about it."

Diana's uneasiness with her new life translated in a terrible emotional turmoil. She became bulimic and was mocked by her new in-laws. What had promised to be a dream was quickly turning into a nightmare.

By June of 1982, Diana had filled her duties as new Princess of Wales by giving birth to a son, Prince William. The continuity of the throne of England was now assured. In 1984, Prince Harry was born, and Diana was no longer needed for any purpose. She had given Charles the two sons he needed to ensure his bloodline would rule over England after his death, and ultimately, that's all Lady Diana was needed for.

Princess Diana was so aware of her manipulated life that she told British journalist Andrew Morton, "Then suddenly as Harry was born it just went bang, our marriage, the whole thing went down the drain."

To the outside world's surprise and sorrow, Charles and Diana separated in 1992, and were officially divorced in 1996.

Diana was granted residency at Kensington Palace to raise her sons, the royal heirs. She was definitely not free from the grasp of the Windsors, but she was at least in a more bearable situation. Over the years, she had grown to fiercely despise her husband. In a tapped phone conversation leaked to the media in 1992, Diana can be heard conversing with her friend James Gibley, a luxury car dealer, about her life with Charles. She said Charles was a real torture, but that she would "go out and conquer the world, do my bit in the way I know how and leave him behind."

While the Windsors did not appreciate Diana's free-spirit (and that's an understatement!), her popularity among the British subjects and the World's citizens grew by the minute. Everyone adored her. She became the Princess of the People. She was kind, caring, devoting most of her time to charities that she championed vocally, and most of all she was real. She was down-to-earth and people could relate to her problems. For the first time in History, there was a Princess who admitted that her life was not perfect, who suffered like millions of other women, who was unsure of herself to the point of suffering from bulimia, who was not afraid to go out in the world and hug strangers, and most of all, who was courageous enough to proclaim all of these flaws, and yet remain dignified.

By all means, Diana Spencer was becoming an increasingly difficult mind to control. For four years, she fought to obtain a divorce from Charles, but the Queen would not allow it as it did not look good. But seeing that the Royal Family's overall popularity was exponentially decreasing as Diana's cause was getting more embraced by the people, something had to be done. The short answer was to grant Diana her freedom and agree to the divorce. But the long answer is more complex, and more gruesome. Accepting the divorce was sweeping the problem under the rug but the problem needed to go away in order for things to go on as planned.

Diana's strength, and ultimately her demise, was that as she grew older, she did not care anymore. She was no longer that easily influenced 19 year old kindergarten teacher. The Royals did not intimidate her any longer. She was now a woman freed from the clutches of the Windsors, and she intended to live life at its fullest.

Enter Dodi Fayed. Or more exactly, enters Mohamed Al Fayed, Dodi's father.

Mohamed Al Fayed was the owner of the popular department store Harrod's Of London. He also owned the Ritz Hotel in Paris, which will play a considerable role in Diana's death in 1997. Mohamed Al Fayed had made a fortune in his native Egypt under shoddy circumstances, in particular via his connections to Adnan Khashoggi, the infamous Saudi arms dealer. This was the stepping stone the resourceful Fayed needed to launch his international business ventures and become a multi-millionaire.

Over the course of his business, he gained the Sultan of Brunei's trust and began brokering deals for him, such as the purchase of prestigious hotels in London, like The Savoy and The Dorchester. Interestingly enough, the Queen of England is actually a personal friend to the Sultan of Brunei. Through this connection, yet another fortunate coincidence, Mohamed Al Fayed met with Princess Diana when she was still in the Queen's good graces.

After the divorce was finalized in August 1996, Mohamed Al Fayed thought it would be in good taste to arrange a meeting between Lady Di and his son Dodi. Did Mohamed get the idea on his own, or was it prompted by his and the Queen's mutual friend the Sultan? We may never know, but this encounter was without a doubt the beginning of the end for Diana.

On a quick side note, it is important to know that the Sultan of Brunei, like many prominent Muslim Elite members, plays a crucial role in the Freemason hierarchy. In fact, the Grand Lodge of Cairo is among the most powerful lodges in the world. If you'll notice, the Ancient Egyptian symbols, such as pyramids and torches, are dominant in the Illuminati culture, not so surprisingly.

In July 1997, Diana was invited to spend some time in Saint Tropez, France, on the Fayed's private yacht. Dodi Fayed, who was engaged at the time to American model Kelly Fisher, arrived in St Tropez a couple days after Diana and started courting the Princess.

Diana was swooned by Dodi and returned to spend more time with him a few weeks later. From this moment until their untimely death, they spend every minute together.

Diana and Dodi spent most of their time in France, between the Fayed's luxury estate on the Cote D'Azur, the Ritz Hotel in Paris and Dodi's apartment overlooking the Place de l'Étoile in Paris. Mohamed Al Fayed was delighted by the budding relationship and encouraged his son to go public with it as soon as possible. Diana, who was now a care-free woman, did not mind the publicity and embraced it with open arms.

Their whirlwind romance became a high profile affair and was widely reported on in the media, and most particularly the gossip papers.

On August 30, 1997, Diana and Dodi arrived back to Paris from a trip to the South of France. They stayed at the Ritz Hotel. Dodi had purchased a diamond ring at jeweler Repossi, across the Place Vendome from the Ritz. Word got out that he was about to propose to Diana. They had planned to dine out at Chez Benoit, but first stopped by Dodi's apartment. On the way out of Dodi's apartment, they were swarmed by paparazzi, who were attracted by the rumors of the engagement. How did they know, unless they had been fed these rumors?

At any rate, Dodi and Diana decided to go back to the Ritz and eat there instead of exposing themselves to the paparazzi.

Dodi spoke to his father Mohamed about the situation, and asked for advice on how to handle the crowd. Mohamed devised a plan that is so out of the ordinary, it sounds dangerous even to the untrained ear. Instead of leaving the Ritz to go back to Dodi's flat using the motorcade they had used all day, Mohamed called a third car, without any escort, and advised his son to go out the back door in that third car, while the motorcade would go out the front, and work as a decoy. The head of the Ritz' security, Henri Paul, would be called back from home (he had been off-duty for a few hours), and he would drive them home.

Here is where things get complicated, and generally unsafe. Paul was not a trained bodyguard, and certainly not a trained driver. Dodi was quoted saying that his father had personally approved of Paul to be their driver for the night. Instead of having their usual team of bodyguards with them, Dodi and Diana only had room for one extra person. This was a bold move, especially considering that it most likely came directly from Mohamed Al Fayed, a man of whom Bob Loftus, the former Head of Security at Harrods, said, "Compared with the protection that Al Fayed affords himself, which is very professional, of a very high standard, that which was afforded to the mother of the future King of England was a Mickey Mouse operation."

So the car they were to use was a small Mercedes S-280, much lighter and less safe than the 600-series car they had been using all day, and it was operated by Etoile Limousine. It must be noted that Etoile Limousine is based at the Ritz, and is operated by the Ritz, fully relying on contracts with the Ritz's guests to make a profit. In other words, it is controlled by Mohamed Al Fayed.

Dodi and Diana were ushered in the small Mercedes out the back door, and Henri Paul, the untrained driver, sped away at 12:20 AM on August 31, 1997. In the car with them was Trevor Rees-Jones, a bodyguard. The car was driven at speed down the Rue Cambon and turned right down the Rue de Rivoli into the Place de la Concorde where it stopped briefly at the lights. There, paparazzo Romuald Rat, on his motorcycle, caught up with them and snapped some shots of the car and its occupants. Rees-Jones was riding on the front passenger seat, and was not wearing a seat-belt, as shown by the photographic evidence from the celebrity picture hunter.

Henri Paul jumped the light, and engaged the vehicle on the Cour de la Reine, alongside the Seine River. He then plunged into the Tunnel de l'Alma, under the Pont de l'Alma. There, the car spun out of control and crashed at full speed into the 13th pillar in the middle of the tunnel at 12:25 AM. This is interesting, because 13 is a recurring number in Illuminati esotericism.

Henri Paul and Dodi Fayed died on impact .Trevor Rees-Jones survived the crash. Lady Diana was still alive after the initial impact, but not for long.

How did Rees-Jones survive the impact? He was wearing a seatbelt. How odd is that? One minute before the crash, he was not wearing his seat belt, as is customary for bodyguards. Yet right when the crash happened, he was wearing his seat belt. Why? Did he know something was about to go down? And more importantly, why didn't he warn Diana and Dodi to put their seatbelts on? Diana was found with her head lodged between the two front seats, which could have been avoided had she worn a seat belt.

Also very interesting is the fact that when you come from the Place Vendome (where the Ritz is located) and you want to go to the Place de l'Étoile (where Dodi's apartment is located), you do NOT go through the Tunnel de l'Alma. Not only is it not the most direct way, it is not the way at all. It is in the opposite direction! So why go that way?

At this point, a car went through the tunnel at 12:26 AM and stopped. Fate would have it that the driver of that car was a doctor. Coincidence? But he was a doctor who, unfortunately, had nothing with him to help Diana. He stabilized her and gave her some oxygen and later recalled that she did not regain consciousness and did not say a thing. His own words contradict later statements where he said that the Princess said she was in terrible pain and called for Dodi. Which is it? Was she unconscious or was she calling for her boyfriend?

Emergency services were called and did not reach the scene for 20 minutes. Now even in a megapolis like Paris where emergency services are kept busy, this is an insanely long response time. There were three hospitals within 4 kilometers, and not one of them had an available emergency vehicle to send to the scene? It then took the ambulance 40 minutes to cover the 6 kilometers to the Pitié Salpétrière, which by the way was not the closest hospital. Add to that the time the medics took to supposedly extract Diana from the wreckage, she reached the hospital at 2:10 AM, one hour and 45 minutes after the crash. She was pronounced dead at the hospital.

When the ambulance arrived at the Pitié Salpétrière, four Professors were waiting for Diana. This is highly unusual, in the middle of the night, to have four professors on call. Surgeons and doctors, of course, would have been more "the norm". But they were supposedly doing their rounds. At 2 AM. The team of highly qualified professors took Diana to an operating room and tried to repair the severed lung artery which was making her drown in her own blood. They tried for three hours before giving up and announcing she was dead. Something here does not add up. The autopsy report said she was clinically dead 20 minutes after the crash, at 12:45 AM. So when she arrived at the hospital at 2:10 AM, she had been dead for one hour and 25 minutes. Yet the professors tried to resuscitate her for another three hours. No matter who the patient is, no doctor in their right mind would work on a dead body, and certainly not on a body that had been dead for over 4 hours, unless it is in a Mary Shelly novel…

And so on August 31, 1997, at 5:15 AM, Princess Diana was pronounced dead in a French hospital.

But what really happened? What caused the accident?
There were reports of swarms of paparazzi around Diana's car that night. Sure, the paparazzi were there at the Ritz. But we're talking about 1997, here. Celebrity hunters were not nearly as common as they are today in 2014. There are actually reports of one photographer near the scene, Romuald Rat, and he fully cooperated with the police. Some say there was a motorcycle that forced the Mercedes to crash into the tunnel's pillars. Others say there was a white Fiat Uno that was following the Mercedes at unsafe distances, at a very high speed. Others again report that a very bright light was flashed from a motorcycle, disorienting the driver, Henri Paul, and making him lose control of the vehicle.

This last theory in particular is interesting if you take into account the instances of mind control by the Illuminati over the years. Let's take a closer look at Henri Paul. Between the end of his shift at the Ritz at 7 PM and the moment he came to pick up Dodi and Diana at 10 PM, no one knows where he was. There is this large blank in his life, and no one has been able to establish where Paul was, what he was doing, who he met, etc. He could have easily been brainwashed into doing the deed during that period of time. This would explain why Mohamed Al Fayed was adamant that Henri Paul should drive the car, even though he was in no way qualified to do so. This would also lend some credibility to the flashing light in the mirrors, as this could have been his "trigger", his signal that it was time to crash the car.

One thing is for sure: it was reported widely in the media that Henri Paul was so drunk, he would not have been able to walk. According to those reports, he was four times over the French legal limit for blood alcohol levels. He would have needed to ingest eight glasses of scotch on an empty stomach to attain that level of drunkenness. Probably close to 12 glasses had he eaten nothing more than a sandwich for dinner. Really?

Additionally, the autopsy report demonstrated that Henri Paul's body showed all the signs of carbon monoxide intoxication. This could not have happened after the crash, since he died on impact. Yet his blood registered 20.7% of carbon monoxide. With a level of carbon monoxide that high in his system, Henri Paul would have been unable to carry on a normal conversation, he would have had hallucinations, and he could certainly not have driven a car. He would have been unable to distinguish his right foot from his left. Yet the video surveillance footage showing him leading the Princess and her lover to the car at the Ritz showed a man fully in control of his movements, showing no signs of intoxication whatsoever. Could he have been injected or otherwise contaminated with a slow-release carbon monoxide poison? Could this have triggered his erratic behavior immediately prior to the crash, such as jumping the light and driving at speeds in excess of 120 miles per hour in town?

And if we take a look at Henri Paul's overall financial situation, it just simply does not compute. Paul certainly had unexplained sources of income. He earned about $40 000 a year at the Ritz and yet he was a keen pilot with 605 hours of flying time at about $500 an hour. He had a string of bank accounts. There were two in a bank outside Paris and three accounts, plus a safe deposit box, at the Banque Nationale de Paris near the Ritz. He had three accounts at the nearby branch of Barclays and one current and four deposit accounts at the Caisse D'Epargne de Paris.

In the eight months before the crash, sums of £4,000 ($7000) were paid into an account here on five separate occasions. In total he had £122,000 ($204 000) and no-one knows where it came from. Enough to appear suspicious. Was he paid to sacrifice his life for the Brotherhood?

Now, the doctor who arrived on the scene first at 12:26 AM reported seeing no one else in the tunnel, thus weakening the theory of a third party involved in the accident. This fact would be easily verified and confirmed by one of the 17 traffic cameras located on the path the Mercedes took that night between the Place Vendome and the Pont de l'Alma. Unfortunately, it just so happened that the city-wide camera system, controlled by the police, was down that night from 12:20 AM until 12:35 AM. Seriously? Isn't that convenient... Even more convenient that at the exact same times, there was a complete radio silence on the emergency channels.

As for how long it took for the emergency personnel to arrive at the scene, and then to transport Diana to the hospital, that entire timeline is ludicrous. The accident was reported at 12:26 AM. The ambulance did not reach the scene of the accident for another 20 minutes. Could it be due to the radio silence mentioned above? When the passerby found Diana in the wreckage, he applied an oxygen mask and reportedly said that she looked OK. Her legs were halfway out of the car on the rear seat, and her head was lodged between the two front seats, on an armrest. Yet the emergency services claimed it took a very long time to get Diana out of the mangled car. Then on the way to the hospital, they had to stop twice due to Diana's condition. And they were not allowed to go faster than 25 miles an hour... How strange is that, when you have a patient in critical condition who, undoubtedly, would benefit greatly of immediate medical attention?

So who killed Diana? And why?

As the Roman writer, Seneca, said, "He who most benefits from a crime is the one most likely to have committed it."

Evidently, the Windsors wanted her gone. Diana was becoming an increasingly greater threat for the Windsors. Once she had given birth to her sons, she was no longer needed by the Royal Family. They had successfully created an heir (Prince William) and their thirst for power was somewhat satiated. Had Diana cooperated with the plan, she may still be alive. But she was stubborn and did not want to be taken advantage of any longer. She started speaking out and in 1995, in an interview for the BBC, she had made it clear that she was privy to many secrets, and was tired of holding out. When pressed further, she refused to say what it was but she clearly appeared distraught. Did the Windsors think she was on the brink of cracking, on the edge of revealing plots and actions that could have tarnished the Royalty?

With Diana gone, the Brotherhood was now at liberty to conduct the Princes' education, away from their mother's influence. When Diana was around, she easily dismissed their beliefs; but with the Princes orphaned, they were now more than ever receptive to whatever the agenda is.

Also, now Charles could marry the true love of life, his mistress of many years, Camilla Parker-Bowles. He could not marry her initially because she did not come from a bloodline necessary to produce an acceptable heir to the throne.

When Diana championed to get to an end of the landmines throughout the world, she unknowingly worried the Windsors. They saw how she was able to rally the world behind her for a cause that many had ignored before. She was powerful and a powerful enemy had to be dealt with promptly and radically lest one begs to be defeated. Henry Kissinger, one of the greatest Illuminati manipulators of the 20th century, met Diana several times. He said in an interview after her death, "She was politically and diplomatically uncontrollable."

It is very interesting that within three months of her death, Diana developed a relationship with Mohamed Al Fayed's son, ultimately leading to her death. One has to wonder what role Al Fayed played in his son's and his son's girlfriend's death. How did the paparazzi know where to find them, when the only person who was in constant contact with Dodi and Diana was Mohamed? Did he tip them off?

Strangely, there was no autopsy done on Dodi Fayed's body. His father invoked Islamic Law that requires for a body to be buried within 24 hours of death. So after a quick external examination, it was determined that Dodi's death was caused 100% by the impact. I guess we'll never know for sure…

One last thing, the Mercedes that ended up being Diana's death trap had been stolen a few weeks prior to the accident. It was recovered stripped, with missing wheels and engine parts. A vehicle that was in such bad shape would have been quite easy to tamper with. It is a wonder the French authorities never accepted Mercedes' offer to look into the crash.

Chapter 13: The Assassination of Muammar Gadhafi

Muammar Gadhafi from the very moment that he seized power was portrayed by the corporate western Illuminati controlled media as a "crazy man" and a "despot", but if you accept these particular claims as absolute truth and fact without further investigation to ascertain whether they are valid or not you surrender yourself to the propaganda and you will never uncover the real reason why Gadhafi was assassinated. So let's take an intense look at Gadhafi and the real reason why he angered the powers that be in the West.

Muammar Gadhafi was born in 1942 in the coastal region of Sirte to parents who were nomads. He studied at and attended Benghazi University, but later dropped out to join the army where he became a Colonel. He came into power in 1969 at the age of 27 after leading a bloodless coup that toppled the regime of King Muhammad Idris who was a so called "friend" of the West. King Idris was considered to be a so called "friend" of the West because he gave the West unfettered access to Libya's valuable oil resources.

When Gadhafi took over the reins of power he immediately nationalized Libya's oil and immediately kicked out the American and British bases that were stationed in Libya which made him an instant threat to the West. As a result of Gadhafi nationalizing Libya's oil the Libyan people standard of living rose dramatically as it was the highest in Africa and one of the highest standards of living in the world. Gadhafi used the oil profits in the following way to benefit Libya and the Libyan people:

- He deposited a portion of the oil revenue in the bank account of every Libyan.
- He built schools, universities and hospitals and made them free of charge.

- He raised the Libyan literacy rate from 20% to 83%.
- There was no poverty in Libya.
- There was no unemployment in Libya.
- The Libyan people were free of debt.
- He raised the life expectancy in Libya from 44 to 75 years of age.
- Made a vow that his own parents who lived in a tent in a desert wouldn't be housed until every Libyan had housing. He fulfilled that promised.
- He subsidized essential food items.
- He enabled any Libyan who wished to become a farmer by giving them free use of the land plus they were given farm equipment, livestock and seed.
- He developed irrigation projects such as The Great Man Made River project to improve agriculture development and move Libya towards self sufficiency in food production.

The Great Man Made River Project

In 1953 while searching for new oil fields in the southern desert of Libya in addition to finding oil Libyan scientists discovered vast amounts of fresh water trapped underneath the sand. Four water aquifers were discovered that each had estimated capacities ranging from 4,800 to 20,000 cubic kilometers. Libyans refer to these ancient aquifers as the "eighth wonder" of the world.

When Gadhafi came into power the Libyan Jamahiriya government used the oil revenues to extract this water out of the desert and bring it to the Libyan people and it was known as The Great Man Made River Project. Consisting of a network of pipes the project extends 4 thousand kilometers into the desert and it involves the pumping of fossilized water from depths of 500 plus meters, purifying it and sending it to the major population areas of Libya. It is the largest irrigation project in the world and was projected to cost 25 billion dollars.

You figure that The Great Man Made River Project would be cheered on and would cast Gadhafi in a better light throughout the Western world, but it did not have that effect mainly because it virtually received little or no coverage in the Western controlled corporate media so therefore the masses of people never knew that this project even existed.

Also, Gadhafi didn't go into ruinous debt with Illuminati outfits such as the Rothschild controlled World Bank and the International Monetary Fund (IMF) to make this project a reality as is usually the case with the so called "Third World" or developing countries. The way that this scam works is these so called 3rd World countries are manipulated corrupted or coerced into borrowing massive amounts of money from the IMF and the World Bank under the pretense of building their country's infrastructure, but what in fact really happens is that this borrowed money is funneled directly to major Illuminati controlled transnational corporations like Bechtel and Dick Cheney's Halliburton and they profit immensely while the borrowing country is systematically bankrupted because they aren't able to pay back these huge loans which was the true intentions of these loans in the first place. Bankrupt the country and when they can't pay back the loans take over their natural resources as a form of payment.

In fact, in his book entitled "Confessions of an Economic Hit Man" John Perkins writes that it was his job working for the international consulting firm Chas T. MAIN to bankrupt these developing nations. He states "I would work to bankrupt the countries that received those loans so that they would be forever beholden to their creditors, and so they would present easy targets when we needed favors, including military bases, UN votes, or access to oil and other natural resources." He then goes on to state that this was one of the methods that the

United States have used and is still using to build its global empire. Now you can start to see the picture of why the powerful banking, corporate and government interests hated Gadhafi and why he was cast as a villain, because he interfered with their way of doing business. He nationalized Libya's oil and used it to build Libya and empower the Libyan people.

Libyan Central Bank

Libya's central bank was also 100% state owned and the importance of this was that Gadhafi controlled and regulated Libya's money supply not the Rothschilds. In fact, in 2000 there were only seven countries whose central bank was not under the Rothschild's control. These countries were Afghanistan, Iraq, Sudan, Libya, Cuba, North Korea and Iran. Is it merely a coincidence that three out of these seven countries (North Korea, Iran and Iraq) comprised George W. Bush's Axis of Evil that he mentioned in a State of the Union speech that he gave on Jan 29, 2002?

Iraq and Afghanistan were of course bombed to smithereens and their central banks were under the tentacles of the Rothschilds. Sudan's central bank soon succumbed and North Korea, Cuba and Iran are presently as of this writing in the crosshairs of the Rothschild banking empire. But what about Libya? I think that you already know the ending of that story. Anyway let's continue to look at why Muammar Gadhafi posed a threat to the Illuminati and the West.

First African Satellite

Gadhafi not only aided Libyans but he was also a champion for a free Africa. He wanted to eliminate its total dependence on the European and Western Powers. Africa did not have its own satellite and was paying Europe an annual fee of $500 million dollars for use of its satellites and as a result phone calls made to, from and within Africa was one of the most expensive in the world. So to solve this dilemma in 1992, 45 African Nations formed RASCOM (Regional African Satellite Communication Organization) so that Africa could have its very own satellite, eliminate its dependence on Europe and slash the cost of communications.

However, RASCOM initially sought help for this project from the World Bank and the International Monetary Fund (IMF). But how could Africa free itself from imperial Western rule if it had to go through the Rothschild controlled World Bank and IMF who charged exorbitant interest rates? Enter Muammar Gadhafi.

Gadhafi put up $300 million dollars to finance the satellite project while the African Development bank put up $50 million and the West African Development bank added $27 million dollars more and that's how Africa got its first communications satellite.

The United States of Africa

It was the goal of Gadhafi to unite all of Africa. He had the vision of a United States of Africa which was the vision he adopted from President Kwame Nkrumah of Ghana. He wanted all the African nations to unite to form one government so that it could solve its own problems. He also wanted Africa to have one army and one recognized national language. Gadhafi was also elected chairman and head of the African Union which is comprised of 54 African states. The African Union was established in May 2001 and launched in July 2002 in South Africa. The main objectives of the African Union were to promote unity and solidarity among African states and to rid the African continent of the remaining remnants of colonization and apartheid.

Of course since the West depended on the exploitation of Africa's natural resources for its survival the African Union headed by Gadhafi was considered a threat to its very existence. To add to this backdrop China and Russia were also competing with the West to gain a foothold in Africa because of the need for Africa's resources to sustain their respective countries. In fact, in 2006 China invited 40 African heads of state to Beijing, China and following a subsequent Chinese visit to Africa huge multi-billion dollar deals were signed on oil exploration and the building of infrastructure. Russia was also working with African nations to advance the cause of Russia.

The United States recognized these new developments and in 2007 George W. Bush authorized the creation of AFRICOM a single Pentagon command for the continent of Africa. Here's what Daniel Volman director of the African Security Research Project in Washington had to say in regards to what AFRICOM's intent was:

"A number of developments—especially the continent's increasing importance as a source of energy supplies and other raw materials—have radically altered the picture..They have led to the growing economic and military involvement of China, India, and other emerging industrial powers in Africa and to the re-emergence of Russia as an economic and military power on the continent. In response the United States has dramatically increased its military presence in Africa and created a new military command—the Africa Command or AFRICOM—to protect what it has defined as its "strategic national interests" in Africa. This has ignited what has come to be known as the "new scramble for Africa" and is transforming the security architecture of Africa."

The African Development Bank

Further angering the West and the Rothschild Illuminati banking cartel Gadhafi set aside 70 billion dollars in The African Development Bank in Sirte so that African nations didn't have to go to the IMF and the World Bank for loans. The significance of this was that Ghadhafi was a Muslim and in Islam usury (the charging of high interest) is strictly forbidden, so Ghadhafi offered loans to African nations without charging interest. As explained earlier the charging of interest and predatory unfavorable loan conditions is how the IMF and The World Bank are able to take control of a country's natural resources by giving them loans that they could never afford to pay back and in turn seeking payment in the form of that country's natural resources.

The Destabilization of Libya Begins

Gadhafi was a thorn in the side of the West from the time that he came into power however the West particularly the United States ramped of their efforts to destabilize Libya and get rid of him. In 1986, President Ronald Reagan ordered the bombing of Libya in retaliation of Libya's suspected involvement in the bombing of a West Berlin discotheque that was frequented by US servicemen.

In the West Berlin discotheque bombing 3 people were killed and approximately 230 people were injured. In the retaliation bombing by Reagan Gadhafi's daughter and several Libyans died. Although no valid proof was offered that proved that Libya was actually responsible for the West Berlin discotheque bombing, Libya was now and forever linked to terrorism perception wise.

Two years later in 1988, a bomb explodes aboard Pan Am Flight 103 in mid air over Lockerbie, Scotland killing 253 passengers and crew aboard the plane and 11 people on the ground. Libya was instantly blamed for this terrorist act and in turn the United Nations Security Council imposed sanctions on Libya in effort to pressure Gadhafi to give up two suspects that were implicated in the bombing of Pan Am Flight 103.

In 1997, after Nelson Mandela made a visit to Libya to persuade Gadhafi to give up the suspects Gadhafi finally relented and in 1999 he handed them over to face trial in a Scottish court in the Netherlands which found one of the suspects Abdelbaset ali Mohmed al-Megrahi guilty and he was sentence to life in prison (but 10 years later he was released from prison on humanitarian grounds because he had prostate cancer). The other suspect Al Amin Khalifa Fhimah was acquitted and returned back to Libya. Once again there was no actual proof given to show that Libya was responsible for this bombing. After Gadhafi handed over the suspects the United Nations Security Council suspended sanctions on Libya.

Seeing how the United States and the Western nations toppled Iraq and killed Saddam Hussein he saw what was in store for him and Libya so he changed his course. He agreed to give up Libya's missiles and weapons of mass destruction. Libya also renounced support for terrorism and accepted responsibility for the Lockerbie bombing of Pan Am Flight 103. In addition, they agreed to pay the families of the victims 2.7 billion dollars. This prompted the United Nations Security Council to lift the crippling sanctions on Libya.

Gadhafi Gets a Makeover

As a result of Gadhafi's "new" attitude towards the West the United States lifted its 18 year trade embargo it had on Libya and took the country off its list of state sponsors of terrorism. The US also lifted its ban on travel to Libya and American corporations began doing business there. European countries also normalized relationships with Gadhafi and Libya. Former Britain's Prime Minister Tony Blair visited Libya to meet with Gadhafi and he and Italy's President Silvio Berlusconi begin to do deals with Gadhafi for their respective countries. Gadhafi's son Saif al-Islam served as an intermediary and a front man in these negotiations. In fact, he was the de facto liaison to politicians, international bankers and business people who wanted to do business with oil rich Libya.

Tony Blair brokered a £560m exploration deal with British Petroleum that allowed it to search for gas and oil and approximately 150 British companies established a presence in Libya once the sanctions were lifted. It is said that the release of Abdelbaset ali Mohmed al-Megrahi was a part of this deal.

Berlusconi's Italy had an underwater Mediterranean gas pipeline that stretched 323 miles in length and ran from the coast of Libya to the Italian island of Sicily. In addition to this, Libya was Italy's biggest supplier of oil and also owned 2% of Italy's largest oil company ENI. It does not stop there. Libya also owned a substantial share of the Milan stock market, 7.5% of the largest bank in Italy Unicredit and 2% of the second largest industrial group Finmeccanica.

The United States not wanting to be outdone by its European competition formed the US- Libya business association which was led by US companies such as Chevron, Conoco Phillips, Dow Chemical, Exxon Mobil, Fluor, Halliburton, Hess Corporation, Marathon Oil, Midrex Technologies, Motorola, Northrop Grumman as well as others.

Neo-con Richard Perle also signed on as a lobbyist through the Monitor Group a Boston based consulting firm to improve Gadhafi's image in the United States. Other prominent figures that signed on with the Monitor Group to enhance Gadhafi's image included historian Francis Fukuyama, Princeton Middle East scholar Bernard Lewis, famous Nixon interviewer David Frost, and MIT media lab founder Nicholas Negroponte, the brother of former deputy secretary of state and director of national intelligence John Negroponte.

Gadhafi and Libya according to his son Saif al-Islam even funded France's President Nicolas Sarkozy electoral campaign in 2007 to a tune of 50 million dollars. Of course Sarkozy denied this. This is what Saif al-Islam stated in regards to financing Sarkozy's election campaign when the tide turned against Gadhafi and the Western powers called for his ouster:

"Sarkozy must first give back the money he took from Libya to finance his electoral campaign. We funded it. We have all the details and are ready to reveal everything. The first thing we want this clown to do is to give the money back to the Libyan people. He was given the assistance so he could help them, but he has disappointed us. Give us back our money."

Why The Illuminati Wanted Gadhafi Dead!

Although Gadhafi opened Libya up to the West and gave up his weapons of mass destruction he was still viewed as a threat to the banking cartel and the ruling elite because of his revolutionary ideas and plans.

For example, I've already mentioned that Gadhafi set aside 70 billion dollars in the African Development Bank so that African nations didn't have go through the IMF or the World Bank to borrow money at high interest rates. I've also mentioned that Libya was one of the countries that didn't have a Rothschild controlled Central Bank.

But the final straw was when Gadhafi wanted to create a new currency called the gold dinar as the new medium of exchange. Gadhafi plan was for the gold dinar to be 100% backed by gold. He wanted African and Muslim nations to join together to create this new currency and use it to purchase oil and other resources at the exclusion of the dollar and other currencies.

This very idea if it was brought into fruition would have shifted the balance of power in the world because oil can only be purchased by countries using US dollars as it is the world's reserve currency. Plus, a currency backed 100% by gold would have destroyed the Central Banks of the world simply because they issue fiat currency which is money that is back by nothing. Libya had 144 tons of gold which was second to only China and would have been a huge power player in the new scheme of things.

Plain and simple, the introducing of the gold dinar would have instantly undercut the United States power. It would have also destroyed the French franc and the British pound. In essence, it would have instantly broken Western domination over Africa and other countries. It is easy to see why the United States, France, Britain and other Western powers wanted Gadhafi dead! John Perkins author of the book Confessions of an Economic Hit Man sums this up succinctly:

"The US, the other G-8 countries, the World Bank, IMF, BIS (Bank for International Settlements), and multinational corporations do not look kindly on leaders who threaten their dominance over world currency markets."

Also just before NATO attacked Libya Gadhafi said that he would no longer sell any oil to Europe. The only countries he said that he would be selling oil to were Russia, China and India.

The Arab Spring

The term Arab Spring was popularized by the Western media and it was used to describe anti-government protests, uprisings and armed rebellions that occurred and spread across the Middle East in 2010. However, documents reveal that so called Arab Spring did not naturally start in the Arab and Muslim world. These documents revealed that it started from plans in the United States to take over the Middle East and its natural resources for the Western world. According to Wesley Clarke who is a retired 4 star General for the United States Army, in 1991, 10 years before 9/11 even occurred it was decided that the United States was going to "take out 7 countries in 5 years starting with Iraq, Syria, Lebanon, Libya, Somalia, Sudan and finishing off with Iran".

To say the least, it was a sinister plan to destabilize the Middle East by any means necessary including covert operations and the planting of operatives in countries planned for takeover as well as the funding of any dissidents. So when the revolt happened in 2011 in Libya everything was going according to the plan that was previously laid out. This revolt, referred to as the so called "Libyan revolution" was fought between forces loyal to Gadhafi and those seeking to oust him and his Jamahiriya government.

The fighting was intense with the opposition forces seizing key coastal cities which Gadhafi quickly reclaimed. The Western media alleged that Gadhafi was bombing the civilian population of Libya and "something had to be done" based on humanitarian concerns. The United Nations Security Council spearheaded by France and Britain adopted resolution 1173 which imposed a "no fly zone" over Libya and military intervention via NATO air strikes and the bombing ensued. The opposition had regained momentum and quickly took back the territory it had lost and they eventually captured the capital city of Tripoli.

Speaking of the opposition forces I find it quite odd that after about 3 weeks of fighting they had the time to establish a new oil company and a new Central Bank to replace Libya's 100% state owned Central Bank. I mean how do you create an oil company and a Central Bank while fighting a war? Even more strange is that they immediately began selling oil right after they captured the Libyan city of Benghazi. The obvious conclusion to these events is that the big money oil interest had a hand in this as the United States and the United Nations gave approval to this selling of oil by the opposition forces. And need I say more about the rapid creation of a new Central Bank? Another country's Central Bank swallowed up by the Rothschild octopus.

Robert Wenzel in an analysis for the Economic Policy Journal had a similar view. He stated the following:

"I have never before heard of a central bank being created in just a matter of weeks out of a popular uprising, This suggests we have a bit more than a rag tag bunch of rebels running around and that there are some pretty sophisticated influences."

Gadhafi Hunted and Murdered

When Tripoli was captured by the opposition forces known as the National Transitional Council, Gadhafi and his family fled the city capital and escaped to the city of Sirte where they attempted to escape in a convoy of vehicles. According to reports a Royal Air Force reconnaissance aircraft spotted the convoy after NATO forces intercepted a satellite phone call made by Gadhafi. NATO aircrafts then fired on the convoy and a US predator drone operating from a base in Las Vegas, Nevada fired missiles striking the convoy. Gadhafi, his son Mutassim and a few others escaped the carnage and fled to a nearby house which was shelled by the opposition forces.

Gadhafi and the group according to a UN report "belly-crawled to a sand berm" where they then took refuge in a large drainage pipe. The opposition forces spotted Gadhafi and his group and according to the same UN report they waved the white flag of surrender. So Gadhafi was captured alive however, he was killed shortly thereafter. A doctor examination revealed that Gadhafi had been shot in the head and the abdomen.

The plot involving the murder of Gadhafi gets even more sinister as several reports pointed to the alleged involvement of the French Secret Services. These reports stated that they had been tracking Gadhafi and that a French Spy infiltrated the mob that captured Gadhafi and shot him in his head. These reports then go on to state that the motive for this was to prevent Gadhafi from being interrogated and revealing his dealings with France's President Nicolas Sarkozy. Nonetheless, Gadhafi was now dead and out of the Illuminati's way for good.

Conclusion

Hopefully, I have opened your eyes up to the real truths behind the assassinations and murders of the major historical figures that are mentioned in this book. There are many other people major or less prominent who I have not covered, but who have also been silenced and disposed of simply because they have opposed the diabolical and sinister plan of the Illuminati to institute its New World Order agenda.

This New World Order agenda in a nutshell consists of destroying the sovereignty of nations, the stealing of the world's resources to feed the Global Empire hegemony, the formation of a one world Central Bank (controlled by you know who) and the enslavement of the masses of people who will not know that they are enslaved simply because they will continue to be convinced that they really do have "freedom of choice" and live in a democracy.

The New World Order agenda will rapidly continue to gain ground mainly because of the ignorance of the masses of people (the 85%) who are brainwashed and are not aware of what's going on. I mean how would they know and understand what's really taking place in the world? Through the schools? Not! Through history books? Not! Through the Illuminati controlled corporate media? Of course not! By watching Keeping Up With The Kardashians? You've got to be kidding me! It's only through books like this will they have a chance to be awakened. So make sure since you've been enlightened that you share the information contained in this book with others. Spread the word. Tell all the people you know about it, because the only way to thwart the New World Order agenda and awaken the masses is through the sharing of information, knowledge, wisdom and understanding.

Don't be discouraged because there is hope, people are starting to awaken and the Global Elite are getting scared because they know that the sleeping giant is awakening. For example, Zbigniew Brzezinski who co-founded the Trilateral Commission with David Rockefeller and is a former national security advisor to President Jimmy Carter in a speech referred to what he calls "the global awakening" that's taking place. Here is a portion of that speech:

'This is a truly transformative event on the global scene, namely that for the first time in human history… almost all of mankind is politically awake, activated, politically conscious and interactive. There are only a few pockets of humanity, here or there, in the remotest corners of the world, which are not politically alert and interactive with the political turmoil and stirrings and aspirations around the world, and all of that is creating a worldwide surge in the quest for personal dignity and cultural respect, in a diversified world sadly accustomed for many centuries to domination of one portion of the world by another".

He shockingly went on to say in the same speech:

"I once put it rather pungently and I was flattered that the British foreign secretary repeated this as follows: namely in earlier times it was easier to control a million people, literally it was easier to control a million people than physically to kill a million people. Today it is infinitely easier to kill a million people than to control a million people. It is easier to kill than to control…'

So what will be the result of this final battle between good and evil? Only time will tell.

Other books available by author on Kindle, paperback and audio

Who Are The Illuminati? The Secret Societies, Symbols, Bloodlines and The New World Order

Made in the USA
Middletown, DE
05 September 2019